DERELICTION
OF DUTY

DERELICTION OF DUTY

THE EYEWITNESS ACCOUNT OF HOW BILL CLINTON COMPROMISED AMERICA'S NATIONAL SECURITY

LIEUTENANT COLONEL
ROBERT "BUZZ" PATTERSON, USAF (RET.)

Since 1947
REGNERY
PUBLISHING, INC.
An Eagle Publishing Company • Washington, DC

First paperback edition published 2004

ISBN 0-89526-060-3

Library of Congress Cataloging-in-Publication Data on file with the Library of Congress

Published in the United States by
Regnery Publishing, Inc.
An Eagle Publishing Company
One Massachusetts Avenue, NW
Washington, DC 20001

Visit us at www.regnery.com

Distributed to the trade by
National Book Network
4720-A Boston Way
Lanham, MD 20706

Printed on acid-free paper

Manufactured in the United States of America

10 9 8 7 6 5 4 3 2 1

Books are available in quantity for promotional or premium use. Write to Director of Special Sales, Regnery Publishing, Inc., One Massachusetts Avenue, NW, Washington, DC 20001, for information on discounts and terms, or call (202) 216-0600.

To my wife and best friend, Nichole, who took a chance on me, endured the White House years with me, and loved me and built a home in spite of my many days away from her. For my beautiful children, Kylie and Tanner, who complete Nichole and me so perfectly. And to my parents, who have supported me and my family throughout the years.

CONTENTS

FOREWORD

BY AL SANTOLI

LIEUTENANT COLONEL ROBERT "Buzz" Patterson is among the handful of United States military officers with the unique distinction of having served at the side of the president, carrying the suitcase containing the nation's nuclear launch codes, also called the nuclear button. In *Dereliction of Duty,* he offers an invaluable eyewitness account of the inner workings of the White House with respect to national security during the pivotal years of the "co-presidency" of William Jefferson and Hillary Rodham Clinton. True to his oath as a military officer—to serve his country with honesty, courage, and integrity—he did not write this book as a personal attack on the Clintons.

Lieutenant Colonel Patterson provides something far more valuable to our democratic process: a compelling insight into the people who were entrusted with the highest national authority at a time when America had arrived at the pinnacle of the world's superpower status. In the most vivid human terms, he describes only those events and decisions having a direct impact on our nation's defense capabilities that he witnessed or of which he had firsthand knowledge.

As a career Air Force pilot and squadron commander, before his retirement in 2001, Lieutenant Colonel Patterson served under

1

four U.S. presidents. He received his commission during the dispiriting era following the Vietnam War, and rose up through the ranks during the revitalization of our military's strength during the Reagan presidency. Aside from his White House duty, he participated in air operations and educating young officers before the "9/11" terror attack on the World Trade Center and the Pentagon.

Lieutenant Colonel Patterson shares with his readers his military background leading to his White House tour of duty, describing his numerous military missions flying into areas of conflict—at times under fire. Serving during a historical period that rekindled America's greatness, he participated in the restoration of the morale and competence of the U.S. military. As a young lieutenant he earned his wings in the Grenada rescue mission under the orders of President Reagan. He later served in the headquarters of U.S. Military Airlift Command during the invasion of Panama and later in Operation Desert Storm under President George H. W. Bush.

As he rose in rank in the Clinton administration's early years, Lieutenant Colonel Patterson further developed the skills and responsibilities of command during the Somalia humanitarian mission—before and after the ambush portrayed in the book and movie *Black Hawk Down*—and by ferrying peacekeeping troops into Haiti. During the gruesome civil war in Bosnia, he was assigned by the Air Force to build and lead a team of skilled aviators to deliver humanitarian supplies into the besieged Sarajevo airport. While the Clinton administration's deconstruction of America's military power was gaining momentum, in late 1995 Lieutenant Colonel Patterson was selected, much to his surprise, to be a member of the elite presidential military aides. From this privileged vantage point, he was able to witness history, controversy, and deceit at the highest levels.

In mid-2002, I was invited by publisher Al Regnery and editor Harry Crocker to work with Lieutenant Colonel Patterson on the format of this book. My own experiences as a combat infantry veteran of the Vietnam War, an author of military history, and a congressional advisor and investigator—part of my thirty-five years of service in foreign policy and defense issues—allowed me to understand Lieutenant Colonel Patterson as a true patriot and an unselfish warrior.

While Lieutenant Colonel Patterson was witnessing the degradation of our national security from the cockpit of U.S. Air Force C-141 aircraft and in the halls of the White House, I was engaged in broader field investigations and participating in legislative counterattacks as an advisor to subcommittee chairmen of the U.S. House of Representatives who served on the Armed Services, Intelligence, Science, and International Relations Committees.

In early 1995, I took a sabbatical from my role for more than a decade as a contributing editor at *Parade* magazine in New York to work in the U.S. Congress. The deciding factor in my becoming part of the government "system" was an investigative report I wrote for *Parade* in 1994–1995, just three years after America's spectacular victory in the Gulf War. At a time when America was enjoying unprecedented prosperity, our finest young men and women, active-duty members of the United States military and their families, were surviving on food stamps and other forms of welfare. Bill Clinton's self-professed loathing of the military had manifested itself in a rapid manner.

In less than three years as commander in chief, Clinton and his subordinates, while increasing the number of overseas deployments, reduced the total active-duty force from 2.1 million to 1.6 million men and women. The Army was reduced from eighteen full-strength light and mechanized divisions to a vulnerable twelve (ten fortified divisions had been used in the Gulf War alone). The Navy was reduced from 546 to 380 ships, toward a targeted reduction of 300—the smallest naval force since the pre–World War II period. And the Air Force was reduced from seventy-six flight squadrons down to fifty.

The net sum of the Clinton years is global insecurity: conflict between the West and transnational terrorists, conventional and unconventional conflicts on four continents, and the threat of nuclear war on the Indian subcontinent and Korean peninsula, and possibly in the Middle East. The Clinton era is bracketed by the 1993 and 2001 terrorist attacks on New York's World Trade Center. The Clinton administration's reckless disregard for America's internal security safeguards led to our country's vulnerability to the unthinkable—attacks on our most prominent landmarks and institutions, on our own soil.

Throughout this period, most military experts questioned the Pentagon's assertion that the United States could effectively fight and win "two and a half" regional conflicts simultaneously. Capabilities were further hamstrung by the rapid elimination of 232 strategic bombers and 2,000 Air Force and Navy combat aircraft—as well as the entire fleet of battleships, essential tools of

American military and political power projection. Beginning in 1994, members of the U.S. House and Senate Armed Services Committees repeatedly warned that the "erosion in our forces' ability to fight" had put the military on "a slippery slope."

In a political sleight of hand, Vice President Al Gore's "re-invention of government" removed 305,000 people from the federal payroll. But 286,000 of those cut, or 90 percent, came from the Department of Defense. Not only were the "drawdown" of the force structure and the severe budget cuts harming the living conditions of the troops, but record-breaking numbers of overseas deployments and poorly planned peacekeeping missions were also wearing down our radically reduced air, land, and sea forces to the point of exhaustion. Unfortunately, the billions of tax dollars and untold military man-hours spent, and the exhaustion of the U.S. military in places like Somalia, Haiti, Rwanda, and Cambodia, showed little, if anything, gained in terms of democracy and the development of civil society in these countries. And in other places—like Bosnia, Kosovo, Colombia, and the patrolling of Iraq's air space—the missions became open-ended drains on our military.

In the July 29, 1994, edition of the *Washington Post,* at the outset of the haphazard relief mission to Rwanda, reporter Bradley Graham observed, "While proud to help save the starving and shelter the homeless around the world, Defense Department officials cringe at the notion of becoming a kind of super, muscle-bound Red Cross or Salvation Army.... Such humanitarian missions are fine now and then, Pentagon officials say. But these operations sap the time and attention of senior officials, cut into combat training exercises, tie up equipment and personnel, and take increasingly scarce defense dollars away from other operations focused on the Pentagon's primary mission of making sure U.S. armed forces remain strong enough to win two regional wars nearly simultaneously."

During that same period, in a warning that might remain as true today as it was in mid-1994, the commander of U.S. forces in Korea, Army General Gary Luck, stated that if a war broke out in Korea at the same time a major battle was occurring somewhere else, such as the Middle East, Seoul and its defending American forces could be overrun before reinforcements could arrive. This concern was echoed by a Clinton supporter, Democratic senator John Glenn: "The idea that we could win in Korea and have our forces [engaged in a conflict] someplace else is very, very optimistic." This security shortfall has not been lost on the ruthless North Korean dictator and his generals, who have more than one million soldiers stationed on—and inside the tunnels under—the demilitarized zone, as well as nuclear, chemical, and biological weapons.

While the U.S. military was attempting to help destitute and war-ravaged peoples in far corners of the earth, a humanitarian crisis was developing on U.S. military bases right here at home. The all-volunteer force had morphed from a largely unmarried martial community that relied on the draft during the decades of the Cold War into a 65 percent married or single-parent all-volunteer force for whom overseas deployments were a familial strain. Making matters worse, in addition to Bill and Hillary Clinton's attempts to turn the military into a gender-neutral social laboratory, morale was further eroded by a military pay freeze, resulting in 80 percent of the total military force earning an annual salary of less than $30,000. The results were devastating.

Thousands of young families, in all branches of the services, applied for food stamps and other forms of welfare—and re-enlistment rates declined to perilous levels, especially in critically needed technical occupation specialties. There were also break-downs in training and a growing difficulty in maintaining high-tech ships and airplanes, and other vital high-tech equipment and weapons systems.

The legacy of the Clinton White House that Lieutenant Colonel Patterson witnessed and reveals in these pages is the degradation of our national security into a state of serious danger. The United States and our democratic allies now face a world where terror and the threat of weapons of mass destruction loom large. The carefree "saxophone, dark sunglasses, and boogie-down anything-goes" attitude of the Clinton administration and the irresponsible arrogance of the co-presidents' cronies and subordinates led to the decimation of America's security forces and our defense and intelligence capabilities. We are now reaping what those years of irresponsibility sowed.

As this book goes to press, nuclear brinksmanship by the North Koreans has become a primary security threat. The origins of the crisis are the diplomatic and security folly of the Clinton administration, especially its disingenuous approach to international arms proliferation and its politicizing of the Pentagon and the intelligence community. The administration's blatant disregard for professional defense and intelligence standards caused

the dismissal or resignation of many quality intelligence professionals and the appointment and promotion of bureaucrats all too
willing to accommodate the Clintons' political illusions. Equally
devastating was a growing lack of respect for the administration—
an administration riddled with moral and political weakness and
corruption—by unrepentant tyrants in places like Beijing, Baghdad, Teheran, Havana, Hanoi, and Pyongyang.

In 1994, when North Korea threatened to turn South Korea
into a "sea of fire," the Clinton administration sent Jimmy Carter
to practice his "smile" diplomacy with the churlish "Dear Leader"
Kim Jong Il. The resulting framework agreement was a fraud;
North Korea did not agree to any substantial verification process
to monitor its ongoing nuclear activities. Instead, through the
agreement, the North Koreans became the largest recipient of
American foreign aid in Asia—among other things, unlimited
food aid for a dictatorship whose militant Stalinist policies were
causing the death by starvation of two million of its own citizens.
And the United States, South Korea, and Japan agreed to build
two nuclear power plants in North Korea at a price of $4 billion.
Undeterred by Pyongyang's history of lying and cheating, Clinton trumpeted, "This agreement will help achieve a vital and
long-standing American objective, an end to the threat of nuclear
proliferation on the Korean peninsula."

For the next six years, the Clinton administration ignored
North Korea's role in nuclear and other missile-related activities
in China, Pakistan, Iran, Iraq, and Libya. The administration's
lack of resolve helped to escalate programs of weapons of mass
destruction in all these regimes. China's missile buildup along

the Taiwan Strait and in the Himalayas adjacent to India, as well as a threat of a nuclear strike on Los Angeles by a senior Chinese general, had little impact on the administration.

Instead, Beijing was rewarded with repeated presidential waivers, including satellite-launching agreements with U.S. aerospace companies that resulted in the perfection of China's People's Liberation Army's intercontinental ballistic missiles. "Friends of Bill" and his commerce secretary, Ron Brown, were rewarded with permission to sell previously restricted military-related technologies to Chinese companies with direct ties to the military. In addition, Chinese companies and middlemen were granted bargain-basement sales on supercomputers, despite the objections of the Department of Defense and other agencies.

Former administration officials successfully lobbied for the lifting of restrictions on sales of powerful American-made communications encryption software. This has enabled the Chinese military to operate its weapons-development projects and conduct military exercises at higher levels of secrecy. In the ultimate coup de grace, the administration transferred the responsibility for licensing sensitive military technologies from a cautious State Department to an accommodating Department of Commerce, which appeared to act as a fundraising arm of the Democratic National Committee.

While the Clintons could favorably impress a substantial portion of the American public, with the assistance of friends in Hollywood, despots around the world took advantage of their self-centered weaknesses. The president's personal scandals and his weakening of the nation's internal and external security capabilities resulted in the loss of trust by America's allies, while earning the contempt of our adversaries. Among many demeaning episodes by the administration that diminished America's international stature, one incident in particular comes to mind.

During the second Clinton term of office, following a period of high tension over the Taiwan Strait, the administration's shamelessness was flaunted before key Asian leaders. It occurred at a gala banquet during the annual Regional Forum of the Association of Southeast Asian Nations, also attended by China, Japan, Russia, and Korea. America's highest-ranking civilian Pentagon official responsible for Asia appeared in a drag costume impersonating Secretary of State Madeleine Albright, wearing her trademark cowgirl hat. He sang a parody of a cowboy song, which included the remarkable line "We don't worry about North Korean missiles because they are called No Dong."

This humiliating performance occurred at a time when regional leaders knew that North Korea was violating the nuclear framework agreement, in partnership with Beijing. Even more remarkable, the administration was spending hundreds of millions of dollars in aid to North Korea, rather than stepping up the development and deployment of effective national and regional missile defense systems.

The nuclear threat goes beyond missile programs; a significant new threat developed during the Clinton years because of the breakdown in internal and external security at America's nuclear development, production, and storage facilities. In 1998, the *New York Times* revealed U.S. intelligence reports saying that China had gained access to highly classified secrets on the most advanced thermonuclear warheads from the nation's national laboratories run by the Department of Energy (DOE). A subsequent investigation by the President's Foreign Intelligence Advisory Board concluded, "The Department of Energy, when faced with a profound public responsibility, has failed."

The failure included the 1998 sale at Sandia Nuclear Laboratory of a $9 million supercomputer configured to undertake national security missions. The buyer was a Chinese national who specialized in exporting advanced U.S. technologies to Beijing. He bought the supercomputer for a fire-sale price of $30,000. According to declassified DOE documents, some department officials belatedly considered the sale a "significant national security concern." Congressman Curt Weldon wrote to DOE secretary Bill Richardson, "Ironically, at the very time the Cox Committee was investigating the transfer of sensitive technology to China, your employees were selling some of our most sophisticated systems to them at bargain-basement prices."

The breakdown of security at the DOE was initiated right after Bill Clinton entered the Oval Office with his commitment to "de-nuclearization." His first energy secretary, Hazel O'Leary, declared an "openness" policy at the laboratories that was, in essence, a dismantling of most long-standing security practices. For example, O'Leary banished the wearing of colored security badges at the national laboratories and DOE headquarters that revealed who had clearances to enter sensitive areas, under the rationale that such practice was "discriminatory." Secretary O'Leary also terminated the standard practice of restricting visits by foreign nationals from sensitive countries—such as China, Russia, Iran, and North Korea—to unclassified areas of the labs. As part of the new policy, no background checks were conducted on most of the thousands of foreign visitors to America's most important nuclear laboratories.

Under the president's declassification orders, voluminous information on the laboratories and other nuclear facilities was transferred from classified to unclassified computer systems, which could be read on the Internet by anyone in the world. Several laboratories complained that providing Internet protection, such as firewalls and passwords, was unnecessarily expensive and a hindrance to operations—and they received a sympathetic ear from the administration.

When DOE security professionals protested the resulting security breakdowns, they were ignored or fired. For example, a January 27, 1997, memorandum from Edward McCallum, director of the DOE Office of Safeguards and Security, reflected the urgent warnings in the office's last three annual reports. The memorandum stated, "During the past year disturbing trends continued that resulted in additional budget restrictions, further diminishing technical resources, reducing mission training and undermining our ability to protect nuclear weapons, special nuclear materials and other critical assets. This is occurring at a time of increased responsibilities resulting from the international transfer of nuclear materials and the dismantling of U.S. nuclear weapons. . . . It is becoming increasingly difficult to protect our nation's nuclear stockpile."

McCallum's concern about the vulnerability of America's nuclear stockpile to sabotage or theft by terrorists—and his frustration at O'Leary and her staff's dismissal of such reports—led to his cooperation with a commission led by former senator Warren Rudman that was initiated by the President's Foreign Intelligence Advisory Board. He also testified before the U.S. Congress. As a result of his candor and dedication to America's national security, McCallum, an Army Special Forces combat veteran, was summarily dismissed from his job by O'Leary's "de-nuclear" DOE executives.

While veteran security officials such as Ed McCallum were conducting heroic back-channel efforts to maintain America's homeland security, a gathering storm of international terrorism was emerging overseas. In this book, Lieutenant Colonel Patterson gives a chilling account in Chapter Seven, "The War on Terrorism," describing an incident in the White House Situation Room in the fall of 1998. America's counterterror network had Osama bin Laden in its gun sights and was begging the White House for permission to strike. But President Clinton had "disappeared" and could not be found to give the order. When he finally responded, he painstakingly procrastinated until the opportunity was lost.

This tragic abdication of responsibility by President Clinton— when action might have prevented the attacks three years later, on September 11, 2001—would not surprise the handful of members of Congress and their national security advisors who followed the rise of the Taliban and the transformation of Afghanistan, beginning in 1993–1994, from one of the battlefields most responsible for the West's victory in the Cold War into the nerve center of the "clash of civilizations" that we now face.

The Clinton administration repeatedly rejected pleas by members of Congress to assist moderate Afghan groups resisting the extremist Taliban and their al-Qaeda allies. Instead, millions of dollars of U.S. humanitarian aid was sent into areas controlled by the Taliban, while the resistance communities—who later became the backbone of the U.S. military campaign against the Taliban—were ignored and their communities forced to accept Taliban control or perish.

Against all odds, in the spring of 1998, the Afghan Northern Alliance had gained the battlefield edge and the al-Qaeda/Taliban forces faced possible defeat. At that time, Northern Alliance commander Ahmad Shah Massoud offered to find and eliminate Osama bin Laden, who had headquarters near Massoud's territory. (Congressman Dana Rohrabacher of California and I discussed this issue with Commander Massoud and his deputies on a number of occasions between 1997 and 2001.) Instead of responding affirmatively, the Clinton administration sent then–United Nations ambassador Bill Richardson to Afghanistan to ask the Northern Alliance leaders to conduct a cease-fire and to stop receiving new arms shipments (from friendly countries like India, Turkey, and Russia).

Tragically, the Northern Alliance trusted Richardson. While the Northern Alliance waited for "peace talks," offered by Richardson and Pakistan, the Pakistani government increased weapons shipments to the Taliban and al-Qaeda. In the subsequent Taliban offensive, aided by Pakistani air strikes and soldiers, the Clinton administration sat idly by and watched as the Northern Alliance was routed. This gave the al-Qaeda/Taliban alliance new life, setting the stage for the 9/11 attack on the United States. Just one week before the World Trade Center was destroyed, al-Qaeda agents assassinated Commander Massoud, the man bin Laden feared most.

Through this book, Lieutenant Colonel Buzz Patterson has performed a heroic and essential service to his country. The reader should remember that the detailed account in these pages is the experience of one man, a professional warrior, tested in combat, who seeks no personal glory and would never intentionally malign any person.

The "Roaring '90s" are over. We are faced with devastating new international challenges that threaten our very survival. To my knowledge, there is no other memoir that conveys such deep professional insight into the unfathomable breakdown in America's security as Lieutenant Colonel Patterson's *Dereliction of Duty*. The lessons within these pages remind us not only of the consequences but also of the essential responsibilities of leadership to which all commanders in chief should be held accountable. Above all, that mandate is a sacred trust between elected leaders and the American people that should never again be violated or forgotten.

Al Santoli is a noted foreign policy analyst, a U.S. Army combat veteran, and the author of the bestseller Everything We Had.

DERELICTION
OF DUTY

A MATTER OF HONOR

I WORKED FOR PRESIDENT WILLIAM Jefferson Clinton from May 1996 to May 1998. I was his Air Force aide, one of five trusted officers who serve the president directly in a variety of duties, mostly sensitive and classified in nature, including—and most important—being the officer responsible for carrying the nuclear "football" necessary to launch a nuclear strike. I arrived in this position filled with professional devotion and commitment to serve. I left disillusioned and disheartened.

I don't pretend to speak for the United States military establishment or its members. I am but one of countless soldiers, sailors, and airmen who have dedicated themselves to the service of their country. But I do speak as a career Air Force officer who had the rare opportunity to participate in combat operations in the 1980s and 1990s and later serve directly for the commander in chief. By chance, I happened to be a man who, in a highly turbulent time in our history, had a front-row seat in the Clinton administration.

I offer a unique point of view. As an Air Force pilot and career officer, I was on the receiving end of presidential directives to deploy in Grenada, Somalia, Haiti, Rwanda, and Bosnia. As the military aide to the president of the United States, I dealt with President Clinton and his chief advisors personally and on a daily basis during challenging times.

In this book, I will speak to responsibility, commitment, and honor. I will speak to integrity and accountability. I will speak to the obligations of command and leadership. And I will speak to how I found these qualities missing in the Clinton White House.

This book is not a personal attack on President Bill Clinton. It will not be a sordid recounting of scandal, personal or professional. President Clinton is a likable person who treated me well on a personal level. If he had been a private citizen, whatever I thought of him privately would have remained private. He was, however, president of the United States. This book is a frank indictment of his obvious—to an eyewitness—failure to lead our country with responsibility and honor. Instead, he led in ways that directly and severely harmed this nation's security and left huge areas of vulnerability that his successor has, in terrible circumstances, been compelled to rectify at speed. President Clinton inherited the most powerful fighting force that history has ever known, on the heels of our country's most decisive victory ever. He left his successor with a fighting force incapable of prosecuting more than one regional conflict at a time and in dire need of reconstitution and resupply.

The soldier's commitment demands that he submit his personal wants and needs completely to the greater good, and in that spirit, I have no personal ax to grind; I have no political agenda; my focus is on the duties of the commander in chief and the basic execution of them that any American should be able to expect. And I know that the greater good was demonstrably *not* served by President Clinton's administration, which put personal wants and needs ahead of the national interest.

As a military man, I was taught the manifest truth that the world is a dangerous place—and I was trained to prepare for these dangerous contingencies, to meet the challenges, and to defend my country. What, in my patriotism and sense of duty, I had not been prepared for was to serve in close proximity to our commander in chief in the White House, on Air Force One, and elsewhere, bearing the nuclear football that was the most fearful responsibility the president bore, and to find that he—the man who led our country and our armed forces—regarded the military with contempt, his duties as a playground for ambition and personal perquisites, and the country as a mass to be manipulated rather than defended.

I do not mean to arrogate to myself the viewpoint of a secretary of state or secretary of defense. But to my presidential aide's eye view, and as a serving military officer who had been sent in harm's way around the world, I was utterly dumbfounded and appalled to see the president treat foreign policy as an afterthought and, apparently, as a distraction that was important only insofar as it impinged on domestic politics and the media. I could regard it only as arrant irresponsibility toward our national security and foreign policy, which, in my opinion, exposed us to the disaster of the terrorist attack of September 11, 2001. President Clinton had not only lowered America's guard to an unjustifiable level but had also established to the world and to those who conducted the day-to-day work of foreign and defense policy that these things really didn't matter, that the country was probably as invulnerable to danger as he was to the many scandals he so successfully dodged, and that really these things could be handled cynically, haphazardly, and on the fly. In the post–Cold War years, it was safe, the thinking went, to play social engineering and vague humanitarian politics with the American military. That this lowered morale and effectiveness distracted the military from its real duty and stretched our troops all over the world on ill-defined, but often dangerous, missions (while sharply cutting their numbers as one benefit of the "peace dividend") didn't matter to the Clinton administration. The inevitable reckoning was horrific.

This book, I hope, explains how one serving military officer saw the groundwork for that reckoning being laid. I hope it is also a warning to the American people that we must never allow the purveyors of such dangerous military policy and irresponsible foreign policy claim the power of the presidency again. I would not come forward now if I didn't think the message was so vitally important to our future as a nation. But as we now fight a global war on terror, we need to remember what plunged us into it. And from my experience in the Clinton White House, I have no doubt of the cause.

I retired from active duty in September 2001. Only then was a book of this nature possible. Since then, hundreds of current and former military men and women have prompted and encouraged me to "tell the story that needs to be told," a story that they know to be true, and of which I was a personal eyewitness in the White House. This is that story.

Mission Aborted

"Eagle departing, South Lawn," crackled the radio in my van. The motorcade wound its way out the White House South Gate, into the streets of Washington, D.C., and onto the George Washington Parkway. This was the scaled-down procession normally used for "unofficial" events. It included a lead police car, the presidential limousine, the Counter Assault Team truck, the Control Vehicle, which I normally occupied, and the black communications van. The obligatory press corps van, or the "Death Watch," was bringing up the rear.

On this rainy Friday afternoon we were on our way to watch the Presidents Cup golf tournament in Lake Manassas, Virginia. It was September 13, 1996. I had been working for President Clinton for three months, but I was already well aware of his passion for golf. Having just returned from three days of campaigning on the West Coast and an early-morning cross-country flight on Air Force One, he was up and at it again. This was the Presidents Cup, the team from the United States versus the world's, and President Clinton wasn't going to miss it.

Shortly before three in the afternoon, we arrived at the course. Clinton, wearing his normal golf attire of a sport shirt and

khaki slacks, was escorted by PGA commissioner Tim Finchem
to a VIP tent area just behind the clubhouse. On the way, he
stopped to shake a few hands and wave to the crowd. The VIP
tent was just outside the clubhouse back door, on a deck over-
looking the eighteenth green. The president was seated under a
protective tarpaulin with other distinguished guests and surrounded by food and drink.

The rains returned, hard enough to prompt a pause in the
action. The president busied himself with an interview with an
ESPN reporter and then returned to the VIP area to be with his
good friend and golfing buddy Vernon Jordan. The conversation
was golf, and the men seemed to be having a great time.

During events like these, I kept close enough to the president
to be always within sight and on call, but far enough away to be
unobtrusive. If this had been an official event, I would have been
in full uniform, Air Force blue, with the traditional silver aiguil-
lette hanging from my right shoulder, signifying the military aide
to the president. Today, I was much less obvious, wearing a sport
shirt with my White House ID hanging around my neck and a
Secret Service pin on my lapel. The obligatory large black
satchel, the nuclear "football," was always at my side.

Though I was called upon to do many things for the president, the "football" was my primary responsibility. Not very
imposing, the football is a hard-cased container, approximately
two feet high by three feet wide, concealed in a leather outer
case. It weighs about forty-five pounds and the military aide has
the option of coupling the satchel to his or her wrist with a sort
of handcuff or a secure loop for security purposes. The football

is the proverbial nuclear button with nuclear launch plans, options, and codes. A military aide with the football is on duty twenty-four hours a day, seven days a week, within feet of the president.

As the rains relented, play resumed, and the president again took his position under the tent. I was summoned to Roadrunner, the black communications van manned by members of the White House Communications Agency. On the phone was Sandy Berger, the acting White House national security advisor. Berger wanted me to contact the president. He needed a decision quickly.

"Major, we're poised to launch air strikes on Iraq and I need the president's nod."

I approached President Clinton, trying to attract his eye as respectfully as I could without unduly interfering in his conversation with Vernon Jordan. He looked at me with a perturbed sigh and frowning eyebrows. Nonetheless, he asked, "What do you need, Buzz?"

"Sir, Mr. Berger is on the line and needs a decision about the proposed attack on Iraq."

"Tell him I'll get back with him later."

I returned to the communications van and the waiting phone. "Mr. Berger, the president said he'd get back to you later." Berger groused and hung up.

These were busy days on the domestic and national security fronts. Just two weeks earlier, on August 31, Saddam Hussein had sent three tank divisions, composed of between thirty and forty thousand of the elite Republican Guard, to capture the northern Kurdish city of Irbil, forcing the mass exodus of from fifty thousand to three hundred thousand refugees, depending on differing United Nations reports.

In the days preceding this invasion, American intelligence officials had highlighted growing tensions between the two main Kurdish groups—the Kurdish Democratic Party and the Patriotic Union of Kurdistan. Saddam Hussein's attack on the destabilized Kurds was Iraq's first major military operation since the peace agreement in 1991—and a clear act of defiance against the United States, since we had become the Kurds' protector. Wary of potential political repercussions at home, the administration was loath to respond to the warnings. Clinton had other things on his mind— namely, his reelection train trip to Chicago, the 21st Century Express, the Democratic National Convention, and the emerging sex scandal of his key political advisor, Dick Morris. Initially, the administration attempted to buy some time with "diplomatic warnings." On two occasions, August 28 and August 31, Clinton fired off "don't do it" notes to Iraq.[1] Saddam marched anyway.

Clinton then authorized a two-day strike at military targets in southern Iraq. On September 3 and 4, U.S. Navy ships positioned in the Persian Gulf and B-52 bombers launched all the way from Louisiana fired forty-four cruise missiles at Iraqi anti-aircraft batteries and radar installations located in southern Iraq. As an added measure, the administration extended the southern no-fly zone north to the outskirts of Baghdad.

While the administration claimed success, the results were underwhelming, if for no other reason than that the Kurds were in the north, not the south. "Our mission has been achieved," declared the president in a statement from the White House.

"Saddam is strategically worse off and knows there is a price to be paid for stepping over the line."[2]

But the real price was paid by those who opposed Saddam. The Republican Guard had executed an estimated one hundred Iraqi dissidents, arrested fifteen hundred more, and generally extinguished whatever opposition Saddam Hussein might have faced from within. Not only did Saddam Hussein claim victory against the United States, but also his antiaircraft batteries fired missiles at U.S. fighters patrolling the no-fly zones, and the Iraqis launched a MiG-25 and a helicopter into the restricted airspace. Saddam Hussein was thumbing his nose at the president. And now, two weeks later, the U.S. was poised to respond again. We dispatched eight F-117 stealth fighter-bombers capable of carrying 2,000-pound bombs into the region and sent B-52s to Diego Garcia, in the Indian Ocean, in preparation for action.

On September 11, two days before the golf outing, President Clinton told a crowd in Sun City, Arizona, that "action is imminent" in Iraq and that "the determination of the United States in dealing with the problem of Iraq should not be underestimated."[3] Pentagon officials claimed an attack was "very likely" and would be "larger and more destructive" than the last set of strikes. Now, on September 13, while the president attended a golf tournament in Manassas—near the site of a heralded Civil War battlefield and the graves of thousands of American citizen-soldiers—National Security Council deputy director Sandy Berger was looking for a decision.

I was called back to the Roadrunner van and took another phone call from Berger. This time he was animated, obviously upset. The attack was to be launched under cover of darkness, and we were wasting valuable time. Pilots were in the cockpits waiting to launch, targets were identified, everything was in place, all he needed was the go-ahead.

These were my peers in those cockpits, fellow Air Force officers and aviators. I could picture them. Mentally and emotionally I could place myself with them. I had been there myself, on the edge of a military operation headed into harm's way and waiting for the chain of command to kick things off. I promised Berger, "I'll make every effort to get to President Clinton as quickly as I can and explain the circumstances. I'll get back to you as soon as possible."

This time, the president was engaged in conversations with several people and was less approachable. I maneuvered through the crowd and caught his eye. When President Clinton saw me, he seemed disturbed at being interrupted again with something unimportant. He frowned as I neared him. "Mr. President, Mr. Berger has called again and needs a decision soon." I explained in a low tone, "We have our pilots in cockpits, ready to launch, and we're running out of the protective cover of nighttime over there."

Irritated at me and maybe at Berger, he said, "I'll call Berger when I get the chance."

Optimistically, I interpreted this to mean soon. Maybe he wanted to find some time, some privacy, I surmised, and would then call Berger. At almost all presidential events, the staff creates what are called "presidential holds," sequestered rooms where the president can relax and where secure phones for classified conversations are stationed. I assumed that the president would find his way to the hold, located in the clubhouse, and confidentially communicate his decision.

Not fifteen minutes later, Berger called me again. This time he was irate—at me, not the president. "Where is the president? What is he doing? Can I talk to him?"

"Sir, he is watching the golf tournament with several friends. I've approached him twice with your request. I've communicated your concerns about the window of opportunity and about the pilots being prepared and ready to go. I'm an Air Force pilot myself, sir. I understand the ramifications. I'll try again."

As I approached the president for the third time in less than an hour, I thought about the hundreds, if not thousands, of people who must have put considerable time and focused effort into this attack plan and were now hanging on the president's decision. I didn't know the details of the operation, but I didn't have to. I knew that we had our military force primed to strike, potentially taking lives, or having their own lives taken. It all came down to a simple yes or no that was being solicited in the midst of a golf tournament.

I made my way through the crowded VIP tent. The president spotted me, headed me off at the pass, and spoke first. "Tell Berger that I'll give him a call on my way back to the White House," he said coolly, indifferently. "That's all." And he dismissed me.

All right, I thought. He'd call from his limousine as we motored back to D.C. The limo was equipped, like his hold room, with secure telephones.

I called Mr. Berger and explained that the president would contact him from the limo. Berger sounded defeated and sighed. "Okay," he said. We both knew what that meant. We'd missed our opportunity.

In the Persian Gulf the sun was coming up. Without word from the president, jet engines would shut down, and pilots would climb out of cockpits and return to their squadrons or beds. Maintenance crew chiefs would put down their headsets and prepare their fighters and bombers for another day. Commanders, war planners, targeting experts, and controllers would push back from their computers, put the phones down, and have a final cup of coffee before heading home.

The president smiled as he signed autographs, shook hands, and waved at the crowd. He climbed into his limo while the staff and Secret Service scrambled into the support vehicles. We made the rainy drive back to the White House.

What haunted me more than anything else was that the president refused to make a decision. Human lives were at stake— the lives of American service members and the lives of our allies who opposed Saddam at our behest and were now under attack. At a time when America's honor and grander principles were being challenged and the world was watching our every move... the president was watching golf.

CHAPTER ONE

AN OFFICER'S OATH

I do solemnly swear that I will support and defend the Constitution of the United States against all enemies, foreign or domestic, that I will bear true faith and allegiance to the same; that I take this obligation freely, without any mental reservation or purpose of evasion; and that I will well and faithfully discharge the duties of the office on which I am about to enter, so help me God.

—OATH OF OFFICE, MILITARY OFFICER COMMISSIONING

MY LIFE CHANGED DRAMATICALLY in late September 1995, when unexpected events introduced me to the White House. I was a fifteen-year Air Force veteran who saw action during many of our nation's foreign combat interventions of the 1980s and 1990s. I participated in the invasion of Grenada and the peacekeeping and humanitarian operations in Somalia, Rwanda, Haiti, and Bosnia. Now I was being given the privilege and opportunity to work directly for the president of the United States. I was following in the footsteps of a long line of distinguished officers. It seemed a wonderfully high point of what many would consider a successful career.

I am the son of a retired two-star general, and I entered the Air Force as a young lieutenant at the very moment when the

Reagan administration began rebuilding the military after the post-Vietnam malaise of the Carter administration. For the military, these were days of resurgent pride and effectiveness.

After twelve months of pilot training, I was assigned as a C-141 Starlifter pilot to Charleston Air Force Base, South Carolina. On October 25, 1983, on only my third mission as a copilot, I received orders to ferry troops into combat, on the first day of Operation Urgent Fury, the invasion of Grenada.

President Reagan had ordered this swift military intervention because of a violent Cuban- and Soviet-backed coup on the Caribbean island that threatened to create a new base of Soviet influence on America's doorstep—and more immediately threatened a group of American students who were trapped at the St. George Medical College.

My squadron was assigned to fly into Pope Air Force Base, North Carolina, to pick up and carry into combat soldiers of the Army's elite 82nd Airborne Division from neighboring Fort Bragg. Our briefing from the intelligence officer consisted primarily of our receiving a photocopied tourist map of Grenada. Our briefers confessed, "We don't know the runway length at the Point Salines airfield where you will be landing and unloading the soldiers. The runway heading is 1-0-0. We understand that it's under construction. There may or may not be trenches dug into the runway. We really have no idea what resistance you'll find. Go for it." That was the intelligence briefing: Here are some guns; there are your soldiers; there's your jet; go. This was the first conventional U.S. military operation in eight years, most of which had been years of deconstruction—and, at first, it showed.

My aircraft commander, Captain Scott Key, and I were armed with small pistols. We had no idea what to expect. The operation was put together quickly and there wasn't time for preparation. As we were about to board our aircraft, an Army sergeant major in full combat gear and with the subdued 82nd Airborne patch sewn on his uniform shoulder pulled me aside under the wing. "Lieutenant," he growled, "just get me down there safely. I've got a silver bullet for the first commie bastard I see."

As our flight approached the island, rain clouds developed over the setting sun. On the ground, the Air Force Combat Control Team, among the first American Special Operations Forces inserted on the island, was coordinating all military aircraft, and the skies were full. The airfield was held and defended by the Cubans, and we looked down at tracer bullets streaking across it. Explosions and small fires blazed along the rolling hills nearby. We circled at 12,000 feet, just off the coast, waiting for the call to come in.

American military aircraft of various types were stacked vertically like pancakes at 1,000-foot intervals. Very little thought had been put into sequencing aircraft by operational priority. Worse, we couldn't communicate with one another. Navy aircraft were on one radio frequency, some Air Force aircraft were on another frequency, and yet even more Air Force aircraft were on a third frequency. We were all in a circular holding pattern over the same point. I hadn't been an Air Force pilot long, but I knew this wasn't intelligent aviation.

At one point, I was number eight in the order, somewhere near the top of the stack. I was carrying soldiers, the fighters who needed to reinforce our Special Operations troops and Rangers engaged in serious firefights. There were airplanes below me carrying less important loads, such as water containers, support personnel, and materials for sustaining the troops for longer periods of time. The Combat Control Team was doing its best, but chaos, confusion, and interservice rivalry ruled the day. I keyed the radio and said, "We've got the guys with the guns but we're number eight."

The ground air traffic control officer returned my transmission and directed, "Mover One Five [my call sign], we need you now. Come on in!" Darkness had set in.

"I can't come in. I've got seven airplanes below me and in my way. We're unable."

Ultimately, we succeeded because of what always happens in our military engagements—American soldiers, sailors, and airmen do what's necessary to make things work. We, the stacked-up pilots, broke all communication security procedures and started radioing to one another.

"Hey, I'm above you and I'm flashing my landing lights. Do you see me?"

The pilots did an outstanding job of not colliding with one another in the darkness.

We decided to make an unconventional descent in a tight spiral down through the middle of the holding pattern. Tracer bullets streaked the night sky as we came in. On our approach to the Point Salines airfield, I noticed on our right an AC-130 gunship strafing enemy firing positions—positions that would have been targeting us. Our airplane was defenseless if not for that gunship.

All around us were explosions and aircraft. But we couldn't let the noise, the smoke, the munitions, and the other aircraft distract us. I kept one eye on the cockpit instruments and one eye on our descent. As we approached rapidly, an Army helicopter cut in right below us, crossing the runway threshold. We missed him by twenty feet or so. It didn't faze us. We uttered a few expletives, laughed out loud like idiots, but kept on coming.

Within ten minutes of our touchdown, our soldiers had completely off-loaded, hitting the ground with weapons drawn and firing. As we climbed back into the night, other airplanes took our place on the field, under fire but doing their jobs.

Scott and I flew two more missions into Grenada during the next few days. The American students were freed without any injuries, the Cuban force on the island was killed or captured, and the Marxist junta was replaced by a moderate government that was secured by a multination Caribbean security force.

Equally important, our military's chaotic but successful lightning operation ignited a renewed vigor among our military men and women to accelerate the new Reagan-era reform that was restoring morale, purpose, and capability.

For the next thirteen years, I was extremely motivated and committed to participate and to lead airmen in combat-related operations. Ironically, my peers and I were involved in more operations during the supposed "peace dividend" and "downsizing" of the military under President Clinton than during the Cold War years of military buildup and improvement under Presidents Reagan and Bush. It was under President Clinton that I saw the greater part of my overseas assignments in places like Somalia, Rwanda, Haiti, and Bosnia.

Even aside from President Clinton's draft-dodging and personal scandals, for which he would have been court-martialed in the military, this combination of downsizing while spreading our military personnel all over the world raised serious misgivings and doubts about him among the men and women who served. Under Presidents Reagan and Bush, our operations from Grenada to Panama to Desert Storm seemed clear-cut. We knew the mission and we knew the endgame. But under President Clinton, our operations in Haiti, Somalia, Rwanda, Bosnia, and elsewhere were much more ambiguous. Or to put it bluntly, most of us in the military thought they were rudderless, open-ended, begun without forethought, and—especially given the administration's defense cutbacks—inexplicable in their frequency and lack of military justification.

A good example of the contrast was in Somalia. President Bush had put us into Somalia in a limited military humanitarian mission to feed starving people. That was a relatively simple assignment—delivering food and medicine—with an obvious end point: leaving after the aid was delivered. But under President Clinton that mission became a United Nations peacekeeping and nation-building operation conducted on the cheap, and with no obvious end point. And it was that expanded mission that ended in the (preventable) tragedy in Mogadishu where eighteen Army soldiers were killed during the ambush portrayed in the book and movie *Black Hawk Down*.

As these sorts of open-ended military commitments multiplied, I felt—and damn near every sailor, soldier, and airman I knew felt—that under President Clinton's command the military was losing its way, doing more jobs, and unnecessary jobs, with much less. Many formerly highly motivated professionals began to think of leaving the service because their missions made no sense to them.

I remember clearly, for example, on a flight to Haiti, during Operation Uphold Democracy, hearing the question "What the hell are we doing here?" asked over and over again. That was the first time I'd ever heard Army and Air Force professionals question the president's decision, and whether there was an achievable mission, a worthwhile goal, or a well-considered strategy behind the entire operation. I'd never seen military members going into a conflict situation so poorly motivated and so poorly informed. That sort of demoralization was bad for the service and, needless to say, bad for the country.

Most of us were doing the jobs we were assigned because that's what airmen, soldiers, and sailors do. They do their best to accomplish their mission. But most of us weren't doing it with the panache we had had serving previous administrations that had given us clear mission guidelines. Criticism of the commander in chief, by all ranks of the military, was new to me—and it was widespread. It could be heard at formal military dinners and at purely social functions with growing frequency. Some even criticized the president openly to the press.

In a culture such as the military, where people are expected to put their lives on the line—without question—for their belief in the honor of their country and their leaders, the fundamental reason for declining morale can be clearly identified. It starts at the top. Whatever moral authority President Clinton may have inherited in the Oval Office he lost very early in his presidency because of a combination of factors. His draft-dodging and his shady past, which came out during the 1992 campaign, were a given detriment, and perhaps could have been overcome after he was sworn in as president. But when his first presidential act involved "gays in the military," when his disdain for the military became almost immediately evident, when he cut the military budget to the point where families of soldiers were relying on food stamps, and when active-duty and reserve units were ordered to more and more overseas missions of apparently nebulous strategic value, the grumbling grew into real and deep discontent.

It is one thing to have a commander in chief you can't respect—and to be honest, most military men and women, in my experience, could not bring themselves to respect President Clinton beyond the formal execution of their duties. But when you couple that with what many regarded as the political promotion of various generals and admirals to top-level positions across the military, then the future can become pretty bleak. When soldiers, sailors, and airmen down to the junior ranks see senior military leadership they don't respect being promoted, they see little reason to stay in the service.

I say all this by way of full disclosure. No officer—no matter how much he tries to distance himself from politics—comes to his late thirties as a political blank slate. Nor does he ultimately waive his First Amendment rights. That being said, I certainly bore no personal or even really any political animosity to President Clinton; as proof of that, I can say that I didn't vote in the 1992 election. He was my commander in chief, and I served him. But I and many of my colleagues no longer felt that our service fully reflected the officer's oath we had taken at the beginning of our careers, and as such there was far less satisfaction in fulfilling our duty under the current administration than there was under the previous two administrations. In short, morale for all of us began to slip dramatically. And that's why, by the mid-1990s, many military people were thinking it was time to go—and I was one of them.

But a summons from the White House was not something I was prepared to ignore. In September 1995, while I was serving at Travis Air Force Base in California, I received a phone call from an office in the Pentagon that handles "special duty assignments" for senior officers. I had been selected from a highly scrutinized list of candidates to interview for the position of Air Force aide to the president. Initially, I thought the call was a prank. But a long discussion convinced me otherwise. I was asked to overnight a package of résumés, officer performance reports, and a photo. Two weeks later the Pentagon called again and told me I was one of the six finalists, which meant that I now needed to expedite the necessary paperwork to go from a top secret security clearance to an even higher level known as Yankee White. I did everything I was asked to do, vowing that when it came to jumping through the many hoops of the selection process I'd make the best of it, present myself professionally, and come home from the Washington interviews having enjoyed the experience of a lifetime. Not in my wildest thoughts or fears could I ever have envisioned actually being chosen for the job.

The interviews began in the New Executive Office Building, part of the White House complex but "outside the gates," in staff slang. I was escorted upstairs to the White House Security Office for the first day of the process, which included the background check and the security screening.

"Is there anything in your background that you haven't told us?" the interviewer asked. "How and where do you spend your money? Can we see your recent tax returns? Is there anything that you're hiding that could conceivably be used for blackmail? Will you agree to a polygraph test if necessary?"

I'm a fairly normal guy and I told them so. I spend my money like most folks, on a mortgage, food, and occasional travel. My tax returns are yours. Nothing outrageous in my background or that I thought would embarrass the president or could be used for blackmail. Yes, I'll agree to a polygraph.

After a couple of hours of detailed questioning, I was dismissed and told I would be called for day two if the initial security screening was judged successful.

The call came, and this time I reported to the East Wing, "inside the gates" of the White House complex.

After passing through the Secret Service checkpoint, I was escorted by a member of the Uniformed Division of the Secret Service—or UD, as they're known—into the East Executive Lounge to wait for my next interview.

Major Darren McDew, the Air Force aide at the time, met me in the lounge and took me to the basement of the East Wing for the first phase of interviews. He was professional and very personable. He walked me into the President's Emergency Board Room, located within the confines of the bomb shelter beneath the East Wing, built by President Roosevelt during World War II and adjacent to the Presidential Emergency Operations Center.

Waiting for me were the four other current military aides: Major Mike Mudd, U.S. Army; Lieutenant Commander John Richardson, U.S. Navy; Major Chuck Raderstorf, U.S. Marine Corps; and Lieutenant Commander June Ryan, U.S. Coast Guard. I sat down at the long, elegant table where the president would sit during a crisis, across from the aides, and they started firing questions. Darren was the focal point of the interview, but each aide took turns. "Tell us about yourself. What are your strengths? What are your weaknesses? What career accomplishment are you proudest of?" All the normal stuff. Then, two very telling questions, I thought.

Darren asked, "Why do you want this position?"

"Well, I don't know that I do. I'm very happy with where I am right now in my life, and to be completely honest, I'm not sure that I'd like this assignment. I certainly didn't apply for it, as you all know, and I'd be just as happy to leave here without it and go back to my position at Travis."

The next question was, "Did you vote for President Clinton?"

"No, I didn't. I'm embarrassed to say I didn't vote in the last election."

"Would you have a problem working for President Clinton given that you didn't vote for him?"

"Absolutely not. I'm a military officer, he's the commander in chief, and I'll salute smartly and work hard for him."

When the military aides were done interviewing me, I was ushered upstairs to the White House Military Office (WHMO). There I had additional separate interviews with the WHMO chief of staff, Air Force Colonel Jim Hawkins, and the director, Al Sullivan. Colonel Hawkins, now General Hawkins, was a great guy and very easy to talk to. We chatted about our Air Force assignments and some mutual friends. It was more of a "get to know you" session than a grilling. My experience with Mr. Sullivan was not nearly so amiable.

Mr. Sullivan had me sit across from him at the small, round table where he was seated. As I bent down, he tossed what I instantly realized was my Air Force career record on the table and blurted, "So, with the exception of your command experience in Bosnia, is there anything else you've accomplished in your career?"

This pissed me off, which I later guessed was his intent. I came right back at him with a list of the professional accomplishments I was proudest of. At one point, he also asked, "Why do you want the position?" I reiterated that I wasn't sure that I did, and would be satisfied returning to my current assignment.

That evening, as I was packing to return to Travis Air Force Base in California, the hotel phone rang. It was Mr. Sullivan's secretary. "He'd like to speak with you," she said and put him on.

"Buzz," Mr. Sullivan said, "I know you told us that you weren't sure you'd want the position. But if you'd be willing to consider it, we'd like to offer it to you."

I was shocked, but managed to reply, "Sir, I'd be honored to be the Air Force aide to the president." Then I sat on the edge of the hotel bed and wondered how the hell this had happened.

I had five months to wind things up at Travis, sell my house, and relocate to Washington, D.C. Major McDew, the current Air

Force aide, was being reassigned to Charleston Air Force Base in South Carolina, but he would have three weeks to train me before he left.

My first walk from the East Wing Gate into the White House on May 13, 1996, was exhilarating. It was a gorgeous, crisp, bright spring day in Washington. My fellow military aides quickly taught me what I needed to know. Along with briefings, advice, tours of the grounds, and introductions to hundreds of staff members, I was introduced to Chief of Staff Leon Panetta, senior presidential advisor Bruce Lindsey, and Deputy Chief of Staff Evelyn Lieberman, the key senior staff in the West Wing, as well as Betty Currie and Nancy Hernreich, the gatekeepers for the Oval Office. I also met the many wonderful men and women who formed the Presidential Detail of the Secret Service, Dr. Connie Mariano and the other great folks who made up the White House Medical Unit, and on and on in a blur of handshakes and hellos.

On my first night of duty, I spent hours walking alone through the Executive Residence and the West Wing. Every corner hides history. The walls—cold, musty, and dank—smell like history. I gazed at the pictures on the wall. I pulled books off their shelves and turned yellowed page by yellowed page, wondering which presidents or famous advisors might have read these same pages. Several of the books were falling apart. One of the first ones I pulled off the shelf was a history of England, and the inscription inside the cover said, "To our new President George Washington."

During my early weeks and months, I was fascinated with the frenetic pace of the daily activity, the constantly busy, energized backbeat. The president's schedule started early in the morning and went deep into the night. Outside, TV reporters conducted their morning and evening stand-up news broadcasts in front of bright klieg lights on the North Lawn. Lines of tourists wound out the East Gate and into the streets. Occasionally, there would be protests and demonstrators just outside the gates. It was chaotic, exciting, and surreal.

The people I passed in the halls were an amalgam of congressmen, foreign dignitaries, celebrities, businessmen, military leaders, and White House staff. In a ceiling corner of my office was an electronic black box broadcasting minute-by-minute updates of the locations of POTUS and FLOTUS, staff acronyms for the President of the United States and First Lady of the United States. This was America's home, the most important building on earth, and I felt overwhelmingly honored to be here.

I had several days of sensitive briefings on the myriad classified programs revolving around the president, and much of my instruction came from the White House Military Office of Presidential Contingency Programs. The responsibilities I would be shouldering seemed so overwhelming that I was numb.

I also met President Clinton for the first time while accompanying Darren on a presidential event in Washington in late May. The president was on his way to a luncheon to make remarks. He was taller, larger than I had expected, with a firm handshake and a warm and gracious demeanor. I was immediately impressed by his presence, his charisma, and the way he looked me straight in the eye. I couldn't help instantly liking him, and was excited to be working for him.

In the next few weeks, I went through a maelstrom of more briefings, more training, and more travel. I accompanied Darren on a presidential trip to Milwaukee and went with Major Mike Mudd, the Army aide, on a campaign trip to Baton Rouge, Louisiana. I merely looked over their shoulders as they performed their aide duties. I attended briefing upon briefing from all of the staff agencies that supported the president, including the Air Force One and Marine One pilots and crew, the Navy personnel that maintain and support Camp David, and so on. It was, in total, a jigsaw puzzle of personnel and agencies. And now I was part of the puzzle. If I had doubts before about the job, they were gone. But new doubts would soon appear.

Chapter Two

The Finger on the Nuclear Trigger

I do solemnly swear that I will faithfully execute the office of the President of the United States, and will to the best of my ability, preserve, protect, and defend the Constitution of the United States.

—Presidential Oath of Office, U.S. Constitution

Article II, Section 1

When the president was home in Washington, we military aides maintained a relatively low profile in our East Wing office. Our presence would be notably visible at state events with visiting foreign leaders, awards ceremonies, and ambassador credential events. When the president had an event in town, we accompanied him, keeping the nuclear satchel by his side. We helped with some of the logistical requirements for in-town events, but most of that was handled by the political staff members and the Secret Service.

I, along with my military-aide brethren, became much more interactive with the staff when the president went on the road. We played a more prominent role in the daily life and decision-making of a trip than we did in Washington. The aide oversaw the large military contribution required for presidential travel

and therefore had a direct line to the president and senior advisors. As a result, we could see clearly into the administration's
day-to-day operation.

My early perceptions of President Clinton, and the development of our professional relationship, came primarily through
our interactions in "unofficial" events. His routine early-morning
jogs and his obsessive golf outings offered me repeated one-on-
one opportunities to get to know him outside the spotlight.

The first nine months, every morning, one of the military
aides had to be downstairs in the doctor's office at 6:30 A.M. for
the jogging detail, which we called "Jogger Watch." The president would arrive anytime between 6:30 A.M. and 9:00 A.M. We
just never knew when he would show up, so we had to be in our
jogging attire and ready to go, though sometimes he'd skip his
jog and go straight to the Oval Office in a suit. He never let us
know ahead of time, so we had to be ready for quick changes.

When he would jog, I was among a small cadre that included
the doctor and the Secret Service jogging detail. I would run just
behind the president as part of the Secret Service phalanx posted
around him. We'd plod about three miles or so. Through many
a jogging morning, the president and I became informal and
comfortable with each other. He started calling me Buzz early on.

These jogging sessions came to an end during the early
morning of March 14, 1997. The president, senior staff, and I
arrived at golfer Greg Norman's compound at Hobe Sound, just
outside of West Palm Beach, Florida, at about midnight. The
president had developed a friendship with Norman and was visiting to play in a three-day charity golf tournament. The presi-

dent dismissed the doctor and me to our bungalow and some sleep after what had been a very long day. Clinton was ending the day with the Normans over a nightcap and would prepare for an early start in the golf tournament the next morning.

Just after one in the morning, I was startled awake by a Secret Service agent banging on my door shouting, "Get up, get up, the president's down!" The doctor and I looked at each other in shock, fearing the absolute worst. We jumped to our feet, and I threw on the closest clothing I could find—jogging shorts and shoes, a University of North Carolina T-shirt, and a blue blazer.

We ran out into Norman's front yard and found the president sitting on the walkway, pants leg pulled up above his knee, in obvious pain. "Buzz," he said, "I think I hurt myself." Major Bill Lang, the White House on-duty doctor and an officer in the U.S. Army, looked him over. "Sir," Bill said, "you've torn a tendon in your knee and we need to get you to the hospital fairly quickly."

Problem was, almost all of the White House staff and most of the support vehicles were miles away in Palm Beach. The staff had chosen creature comforts over proximity and potential presidential contingency, and was nowhere near the Norman compound. As a result, the Secret Service agents, Bruce Lindsey, the doctor, and I quickly assembled a makeshift motorcade of rental cars, gingerly placed the president into an awaiting ambulance, and motored off to the hospital some forty-five minutes away.

If the president's injury had been any more serious, it wouldn't have been funny. But the whole episode was a bit comical, given that the president's injury appeared to be the result of having a bit too much to drink. The lead Secret Service agent led the procession at high speeds down dark beachside roads in his rental car. I threw myself in the back of the Counter Assault Team's black truck, head over heels, and started the emergency notification process over my cell phone. There's not a lot of cell phone connectivity on roads along the beach in rural eastern Florida. Through lack of forethought on all of our parts, there were no secure communications, no protective cover of presidential limousine, no police escort.

Later that morning, after several hours at a Palm Beach hospital, we would all board Air Force One and fly back to Bethesda, Maryland, for the president's surgery. His jogging days, as the president, were over.

Typically, members of the White House staff concerned themselves with media reaction and media complaints that they had not been expeditiously notified about the president's condition. The real—and ignored—news here was the lack of readiness and response for a president who could have been seriously injured. The military aides and Secret Service sat down after the debacle and made arrangements to prevent such a future occurrence. The staff worked the media spin, while we handled the facts. That was the usual division of labor.

The president also took his golf seriously and seized any opportunity to sneak away and play eighteen holes. Like the "jogger-cades," the golf events required the attendance of the Secret Service, the doctor, and the military aide. We'd saddle up our golf carts and follow the president and invited guests around the course for the four-hour vigil. These outings could be "working" events with politicians such as Senator John Kerry or Senator Chris Dodd, or with campaign donors and businessmen. Or they could be solitary efforts, with the president just trying to get in a quick eighteen holes. In any event, they offered me occasions to share time with President Clinton and come to know the man.

My first inklings into the makeup and personality of Bill Clinton and those he surrounded himself with came during these golf outings. Much has been made of his propensity to cheat or to stretch the truth. Even in these inconsequential golf games, he would cheat with ball placements and extra shots. The way he played golf, I came to understand, was not just a peccadillo but symptomatic of the way he approached life.

During the presidential vacation to Martha's Vineyard in August 1997, the White House doctor and I decided to document, just for fun, the president's scoring transgressions. Using the cardboard lid from a boxed lunch the White House valets had prepared for the outing, we secretly kept President Clinton's score. Hole after hole, we noted his actual score. At the end of the course, we were able to sneak his scorecard from his golf cart and compare it with the scores we had kept. Sure enough, when the press interviewed him following his round, he claimed he shot a 79. Actually, it was a 92.

I became more comfortably involved in the daily life in the Clinton White House. As a newcomer I asked for a White House organizational chart, a wiring diagram, something that laid out the administration's chain of command. I was told, "There isn't one." That didn't entirely surprise me, because the Clinton White House seemed disjointed, reactive, and highly undisciplined to a career military officer. In Air Force flying parlance, we'd term this "all thrust, no vector" or "all fluff, no stuff." I searched the files in the Military Aide's Office for White House regulations, continuity folders, and guidelines and found very little. The best I could do was an office phone listing.

Dee Dee Myers, President Clinton's first press secretary, observed early on in the administration, "It was very clear to me right away that we were making this up as we went along. There was no instruction manual."[1] Things hadn't changed by the time I got there, because watching the White House staff gave me the very same impression Dee Dee Myers had. You wouldn't run an Air Force base this way, and I found it hard to accept—in fact I never did—that this was how the most important building in the world was run. The unofficial bywords of the administration's culture were confusion, inefficiency, mayhem, and dysfunction. But at the same time, the political machine was impressive, even if crisis-oriented in nature; it was obviously committed to the president, and the energy level was high.

Every morning, staffers would scour the overnight news and morning headlines of major newspapers across the country. Brewing scandals, crises, and criticisms would rule the day. If there was a fire to be put out, it became the priority. If there had been a politically damaging attack from the Right, a counter-attack was planned. "When can we have the president make a statement?" comments were murmured through the halls. Tactically, the staff was in its element, but there was no strategic vision that I could see.

Another shortcoming was dishonesty—not just about golf and extramarital affairs but also about our national security. Such dishonesty said much about the president's priorities. On August 26, 1996, just three months into my tenure, I was accompanying the president in Toledo, Ohio, on one of his many reelection campaign events. I listened to his speech from one of the "hold" rooms offstage. Television images and sound were piped into the room by the White House Communications Agency. I heard President Clinton say, "For the first time since the dawn of the nuclear age, on this beautiful night, there is not a single nuclear missile pointed at a child in the United States of America."[2]

I looked down at the black satchel at my side. "What?" I mumbled out loud. I turned to the military White House doctor along on the trip and asked him, "Did he just say what I think he said?" The doctor shrugged and nodded. It was patently untrue, and anyone with a remote knowledge of military and foreign affairs knew it was untrue.

There were missiles clearly pointed at us and we were pointing missiles at others. The military aides had briefed the president annually on the specifics, and I was carrying the satchel full of the details. That autumn, I heard him deliver the line in speeches again and again and again. President Clinton made this claim more than 130 times during the 1996 reelection campaign alone.[3] It left me slack-jawed that one of his major campaign themes could be such an obvious, whopping lie.

But on another level it didn't surprise me, because almost daily I was privy to high-level conversations among the president's senior staffers—people like Bruce Lindsey, Sandy Berger, one-time deputy chief of staff and political advisor Harold Ickes, senior advisor Rahm Emmanuel, deputy chief of staff, and later chief of staff, John Podesta, and others who would travel with us in the motorcades. The conversation was not on the sort of strategic policy issues that someone with my background would expect a group of senior advisors to discuss with the commander in chief. No, the focus was squarely on such topics as subpoenas, executive privilege, and how and when to make press statements. Where I expected a focus on strategy—just as I would expect it in conversations of senior military leaders—I instead found spin and almost nothing but spin.

Prior to my arrival at the White House, I had heard about the various scandals and the accusations directed at the Clintons. I remembered Clinton during his first campaign pronouncing that his would be the "most ethical administration in history." I knew of the accusation of adultery and the Whitewater dealings that predated his election to office. I had heard about the issues of FBI files, the Travel Office fiasco, and, of course, the death of Vince Foster that had arisen since. The sheer variety of the charges amazed me. The litany of Clinton scandals that every American had read or heard about since his 1992 presidential campaign now came vividly alive for me, as scandal reaction was a central concern of the Clinton administration.

And the most damning aspect, for me as an eyewitness, of the continual priority given to spin over substance concerned the nuclear "football" of which I was one of the guardians.

On January 17, 1998, the president was compelled to confront the Paula Jones lawsuit. On that day, the president gave his deposition in the offices of his attorney just blocks from the White House. I attended as part of the presidential entourage. I was sequestered in an office down the hall, while the president spent hours testifying. At one point, I met Bruce Lindsey in the men's room and asked, "How's it going, sir?"

Bruce Lindsey, White House counsel, "presidential best friend," was the keeper of the skeletons in the president's closet. I liked Bruce. Of all the senior staff, he was one of the friendliest and most knowledgeable about what was really going on.

Lindsey, looking very tired and drawn, replied, "About as well as can be expected, I guess."

Four days later, on January 21, I was the first person on President Clinton's schedule. At seven in the morning, I was going to give the president his annual nuclear update briefing and his new set of nuclear "go codes."

I arrived early, notes in hand, anxious to instruct him and answer his questions. It was the last event on my rota of twenty-four-hour duty at the White House.

I walked into the Oval Office's outer area, the office of Betty Currie. Betty wasn't in yet, but Kris Engskov, the president's personal aide, met me and advised me to wait.

I walked over to Betty's desk and glanced down at the morning's *Washington Post*. The headline was "Clinton Accused of Urging Aide to Lie: Starr Probes Whether President Told Woman to Deny Alleged Affair to Jones's Lawyers."[4]

I had heard rumors about the president conducting an illicit affair with a young intern. I'd even seen the intern once or twice, and asked a colleague what she was doing in the West Wing. I was told to leave it alone. Now I knew why.

Kris motioned me into the Oval Office. Clinton was seated behind his desk. He looked tired and beaten, blanched and swollen. He looked up at me from behind his reading glasses.

"Sir, if you'd like, we can just change out the codes now and I'll come back for the briefing later."

"That'd be fine, Buzz. Thank you."

I handed him the new card—the biscuit, we called it—with the new codes, which would be effective immediately. One of the most important symbols of military power in the history of man had just exchanged hands. He looked back down at his desk and the morning newspapers piled in front of him. I was waiting for him to respond in kind. He didn't offer me his old set of codes, however, and I figured now was not a good time to press the issue. I showed myself out of the office and returned to the East Wing.

After the Lewinsky affair broke, the senior staff tried to insulate the president from further problems. Their intent was to keep him "safe" from women. With the president's help, the staff developed a code word for attractive females: they called them "security risks." In my opinion, they weren't the only "security risks."

The biggest security risk was the president himself.

When one of the other military aides and I returned, a few days later, to brief the president on changes to the contents—and the launch codes—of the football, we were in for a surprise. We arrived at the Oval Office as scheduled. My military-aide compatriot briefed the president on the important changes. My expectation was that the president would finally return his old set to us. Instead, President Clinton looked up sheepishly and confessed, "I don't have mine on me. I'll track it down, guys, and get it back to you."

We were dumbfounded—*the president losing his nuclear codes.* He is required to have the codes on him at all times. President

Clinton normally kept the world's most sensitive document rubber-banded to his credit cards in his pants pocket.

There had been one other time that he had misplaced the codes, but we were able to quickly track them down through his valets. He'd left them in the White House residence while he was leaving for a round of golf. This time, though, the codes were apparently lost.

It is true that once before President Reagan had been separated from his codes during the attempt on his life. The FBI had seized the contents of his pockets for their investigation of the assassination attempt. Quickly, the White House retrieved them and returned them to the president. Also, President Carter once accidentally sent his to the cleaners in the pocket of a suit. Again, he immediately notified his aides, and they were retrieved without delay.

In this instance, though, there was a pregnant pause, and then the president merely went back to work on the pile of papers in front of him. As we left, we couldn't help wondering how long the codes had been missing.

We immediately alerted the Joint Staff in the Pentagon. "What do you mean? How could this happen? You've got to find it ASAP!" They were incredulous.

For days, we turned over everything in the White House. We talked to the ushers and valets, and asked them to search the president's clothes and furniture in the residence. We asked the senior staff, specifically John Podesta and Bruce Lindsey, for help.

The president finally threw up his hands and said casually, "I just can't find it...don't know where it is." As far as he was concerned, that was the end of the story; Podesta and Lindsey's overriding concern was that the story might leak to the press. Only the military seemed remotely worried about the national security implications of the nuclear launch codes' being lost. And they were never found.

During NATO's Fiftieth Anniversary summit in Washington, D.C., on April 24, 1999, President Clinton departed the meeting in such a rush that he left his military aide and the nuclear football behind. There was some discussion among the staff that not everyone had been marshaled for the motorcade back to the White House. The president wasn't in the mood to wait...and he left. The befuddled aide, my successor, didn't know what to do. This was the first time it had ever happened. Rather than take his chances with public transportation, he walked, in spit-and-polished uniform, and football in hand, several blocks back to the White House.

For thirty or forty minutes, the president and the nuclear football were separated. The president had made that conscious decision and couldn't be bothered to wait the additional minute or so to ensure that his entire entourage, especially the essential foreign policy element, could come along. "Rather than wait for everyone, he just took off," said press secretary Joe Lockhart.

This is the Clinton administration I knew.

CHAPTER THREE

HILLARY'S "FOOTBALL"

Hell is murky!—Fie, my lord, fie! a soldier, and afeard? What
need we fear who knows it, when none can call our power to
account?

—*MACBETH*, ACT 5, SCENE 1

AMONG THE MILITARY WHO SERVED in the White House and the
professional White House staff, the Clinton administration was
renowned for its lack of professionalism and courtesy, though
few ever spoke publicly about it.[1]

This aspect of the Clinton administration became apparent to
me from my earliest golf outings with the president. It was telling
to me how often he played golf with certain types of people—
people like Terry McAuliffe, his campaign and fundraising guru,
and the Rodham brothers, Hugh and Tony. They, like many of
Clinton's cronies, were remarkably pompous and inconsiderate
individuals. The Rodham brothers are characters right out of *The
Sopranos,* and they took full advantage of the fact that they were
the first lady's brothers. They were loud, obnoxious, demanding,
and rude, and treated the military aide and the support staff as
glorified caddies. They assumed that since we were there to assist
the president, we were also there to serve them. They would think

nothing of asking and expecting an Air Force or Army colonel to carry their golf bags for them. It was a perk of being a friend of Bill, a brother of Hillary. This might seem an inconsequential point, but it set a consistent tone to the administration, and in my mind it was impossible, over time, not to fit it into a larger picture. These people—McAuliffe and the Rodhams and so many other Clinton cronies—were people who regarded the Clintons' electoral success as all about them and what they could get out of it. One significant exception to the sort of behavior we learned to expect from "friends of Bill" was White House chief of staff Erskine Bowles. He was a gentleman, and kindly admonished me when I tried to carry his clubs: "I'm ex–Coast Guard enlisted; no military officer is going to carry my clubs."

With others, however, the arrogance and pomposity spilled beyond an antimilitary attitude into what appeared to be a racist attitude. President Clinton surrounded himself with minority cabinet members and celebrities, and devoted countless speeches and statements championing diversity, but some of the most racially prejudiced behavior I have ever experienced happened at the Clinton White House. I can only assume it was driven as much by sheer bad manners as by implicit racism. One cabinet member who struck me as particularly racist was Secretary of Labor Alexis Herman, herself an African-American woman. She treated the young African-American enlisted men who drove for the White House Transportation Agency like second-class citizens. And she had no qualms about ordering an African-American Navy officer who carried the presidential medical supplies, such as the defibrillator and plasma, to carry her luggage on and off the plane as well. This Navy officer's primary duty was to ensure that nothing happened to the president, and in the event that something did, to tend to his medical needs. But to Alexis Herman, he was just another flunky at her disposal. I could see the hurt in his eyes; he expected more. And I felt for him. I was stunned to find that friends of Bill, like Jesse Jackson, treated African-American White House staff in the same way. This was an alien concept to me. The armed forces have spent decades overcoming racial divisions and inequities. Our standard now is based solely on merit and rank. On the other hand, it seemed to be a habit among some of Bill's high-profile friends and colleagues that when outside of public purview they reflexively treated African-American service members in a manner I found appalling.

During the reelection campaign of 1996, we were visiting Tampa, Florida. As we departed Air Force One and the Tampa airport via motorcade, we passed directly in front of the Tampa Bay Buccaneers professional football team complex. Many of the players and coaches were outside, taking a break from practice, and watched in awe as the enormous presidential motorcade snaked by. President Clinton, quick to realize an opportunity when he saw one, had the motorcade turn around and return to the Bucs' football facilities. The press corps was in tow, and this would make for a great off-the-record political news moment.

As we piled out of the vehicles, the president went from player to player, coach to coach, and shook hands. Tampa Bay head coach Tony Dungy, a dignified black man, a former professional player himself, and one of only a few African-American head coaches in the NFL, stood close by me and we chatted informally. At that moment, one of the senior white female staff members approached. She looked over our heads and around the scene, obviously looking for an older, white man, an "authority figure," when she asked Mr. Dungy, "Can you tell me where the head coach is?" Chagrined for the staff, I told her, "You're talking to him." Dungy was a gentleman and handled it well, but even so, the senior advisor was unaffected. She just walked away, seemingly no remorse felt, and certainly no apology given.

As much play as the media gave to the Bill Clinton–Jesse Jackson relationship, that arrangement also struck me as somewhat disingenuous. The president liked to refer to himself, as a writer had done, as the nation's "first black president." His actions, at least those that I could see, spoke otherwise. Many times, Reverend Jackson would try to place calls to the president. The military aide would be the call screener at places like Camp David, on the golf course, on vacation, wherever normal White House staff and operators were unavailable. I'd put the caller on hold, ring the president, and ask, "Sir, it's so-and-so. Do you want me to put them through?" Almost without exception, Clinton would refuse calls from Jackson. I can't tell you how many times I had to tell Mr. Jackson that the president was unavailable and would have to get back to him. Most of the time, he never did.

But when it came to rudeness and such, it was Hillary Clinton who was the most feared woman in the administration.

When I first met Mrs. Clinton, it was on Marine One headed for Camp David, and I confess I was nervous. The other military aides had warned me, "Whatever you do, don't piss off the first lady." The first couple had notorious tempers, but hers was the worst. She was the one who could rip your heart out.

She was guardedly gracious and warm as she held out her hand and said, "Major Patterson, Hillary Clinton. It's nice to meet you."

"Hello, ma'am, Buzz Patterson. It's a pleasure to meet you."

In turn, she introduced me to Chelsea seated across from her on the couch in the helicopter's distinguished rear compartment. Designed for the first family, Marine One had large leather chairs for the president and first lady, and couch seats lining each side of the rear compartment. Chelsea, hair pulled back, in blouse and blue jeans, was polite and quiet.

The protocol on Camp David trips was that the military aide accompanied the first family as part of a small retinue. In addition to our normal responsibilities, we assumed the duties typically held by the personal aide, secretary, and valet. As such, I helped load the family luggage onto and off the helicopter. I helped them get situated into "Aspen," their Camp David cabin, and I stood by for anything that they might need to complete their daily schedules.

One of my fellow aides, a Camp David veteran, advised me, "Make sure you put Mrs. Clinton's luggage in their bedroom specifically where she wants it." And I quickly knew how right he was after I shook the first lady's hand and she introduced me to Chelsea on Marine One. I noticed that she was visibly concerned about her many hatboxes and bags. Judging from Hillary's laser-like attention, the most important piece of luggage was a plastic box of files. My compatriot had instructed me, "Only you [the military aide] should handle the files and only in the presence of Mrs. Clinton. Place them beside her on Marine One. When you get to Camp David, place the files in a conspicuous location in her bedroom. Make sure that she sees you when you're moving them and she sees exactly where you leave them."

Pretty significant box of files, I thought. I never knew exactly what these files contained, but as events unfolded over the next several months, I developed strong suspicions. Earlier in the year, some long-subpoenaed Rose Law Firm Whitewater billing records had surfaced in the residence after two years of absence. Now Senate investigators were asking Mrs. Clinton for more information concerning her handling of Vincent Foster, Castle Grande, and Rose Law Firm records. Concurrently, there were House hearings into the improper collection of FBI background files and an ongoing legal battle over documents related to the Travel Office firings. Whatever files these were, they were important luggage.

And she was hawklike about it. That opaque plastic file box never left her sight. Whenever she left the White House, those files—the handling of which, in her opinion, was the chief responsibility of the military aide—went with her. One of my colleagues warned me early on, "Don't screw up those files. Those files need to get to where she wants them, now, ASAP—they are very important."

I learned very quickly that the administration's day-to-day character, whether inside or outside Washington, depended on the presence or absence of Mrs. Clinton. Her personality preceded her. As part of my early training, I was told by my predecessor that "when Mrs. Clinton is 'moving' through the halls, make yourself as inconspicuous as possible." The general advice was that Hillary did not want to see the staff, with the exception of key senior members, in the halls of the White House. Many a time, I'd see mature, professional adults scurrying into office doorways to escape Mrs. Clinton's line of sight. I'd hear whispered, "She's coming, she's coming." I could be walking down a West Wing hallway, midday, and find people busier than hell doing the administration's work in the press office, medical unit, wherever. She'd come in, and they'd scatter. She was the stern schoolmarm, and the rest of us were expected to hide as though we were kids in trouble. It was ridiculous but understandable. Hillary could be harsh, difficult, and unpredictable.

Our trips to Camp David were a case in point. Camp David is run by the military, and it was our job, as military aides, to notify the commander and his staff of first-family visits. We were also counted on to alert key support agencies such as the Secret Service, the White House Communications Agency, the White House Medical Unit, and the valets. And we were to arrange the transportation with Marine One. The trouble was that Hillary's staff would not communicate with us.

One of my fellow military aides got caught in this Hillary trap. He spent days trying to confirm rumors of a trip. On Friday night, after exhausting all available sources, he finally concluded that there wasn't going to be a trip this weekend. On Saturday morning, early, Mrs. Clinton called him. "Where are the helicopters? Where is Marine One? I'm ready to be picked up," she demanded.

"Ma'am, we need two hours, minimum, to arrange the logistics and you're giving me fifteen minutes." In Hillary fashion, she snapped, "You were told last night," and she slammed the phone down.

My compatriot jumped to and made the necessary arrangements. In minutes, Marine One rotors were spinning and en route to the South Lawn. The Secret Service, Camp David staff, White House Medical Unit, White House Communications Agency, and Press Office all received rushed "we're going" phone calls and went into their own crisis modes. That was standard operating procedure from Hillary's staff. And it was not necessarily the staff's fault.

Kelly Craighead was Hillary's personal aide while I was there. It was an unenviable position. Her boss gave her frequent tongue-lashings along the lines of "You didn't tell me this person was going to be at the social event," or "Kelly, I'm late for this and I shouldn't be late," or "Kelly, this dress is the wrong color for this event." The words were snapped with a distinctive, bitter nastiness. She was like that with people in her inner circle.

In early January 1997, the Clintons and entourage were going to St. Thomas, the Virgin Islands, for a vacation. The trip had been planned for weeks and most of the logistics were set. But as soon as Air Force One touched down in St. Thomas, I knew something was amiss. Mrs. Clinton was visibly upset. The staff quickly learned that Chelsea had left her backpack full of books in Hilton Head, South Carolina, where the Clintons had been attending their annual Renaissance Weekend, a gathering of government, business, media, and academic leaders. But it wasn't Chelsea's fault, of course, because, according to Hillary, the valets were to blame.

The president is served by career Navy enlisted men as valets. These valets, Filipino by birth, have a long, proud tradition of serving the first family. In my experience, they were loyal, devoted, impeccable employees. They worked diligently to attend to every detail—no matter how small.

It seemed to me amazing that the idea of holding Chelsea responsible—Chelsea was a senior in high school—never crossed Hillary's mind.

Kelly Craighead asked me to find a way to get the books down to St. Thomas *tout de suite*. Chelsea had finals approaching and needed to study. We sprang into crisis mode. I called back to Hilton Head, catching my fellow milaide before she caught her return flight to Washington. She sounded the alarm, gathered remaining White House staffers, and scurried to find the backpack. Once the backpack was safely in hand, we dispactched one of the president's valets via commerical airliner to deliver the goods. Just another day in the Clinton White House—the quick assignment of blame, and a relatively minor issue mushrooming quickly out of control.

The president's mood also greatly depended on the presence or absence of Hillary. When she wasn't around, he had more fun. He played golf and played cards with Lindsey, Podesta, or Bowles. He'd stay up to all hours of the night smoking cigars and talking to anyone who'd listen. When she was along, he toed the line. He was on time and he'd go to bed. He feared her, it seemed.

Within my first few months, I witnessed just how intense her fury at her husband could be. We were on our way to a Washington fundraising event. I knew it was going to be a bad night when the limousine pulled up at the hotel and there was a long delay before the first couple stepped out. They were arguing in the backseat.

Finally, the president, the first lady, two Secret Service agents, the doctor, and I crowded into the loading dock elevator to reach the party at the top of the hotel. Mrs. Clinton had just received some bad news about the Whitewater investigation and her immunity. As soon as the elevator door closed, she exploded at the president with a spew of four-letter words.

Every vulgar word you've ever heard poured from her mouth: "Goddammit," "you bastard," "it's your fucking fault." On and on and on. What grabbed my attention was not so much that she was saying these things but the way the president reacted. He looked like a beaten puppy. He put his head down and didn't try to fight back. He said, "Yes, I understand. Yes, dear, I know." The rest of us weren't supposed to make eye contact anyway, so I blended in with the carpeted walls of the elevator and avoided the alarmed glances of the doctor and agents. The president, embarrassed, placated her as best he could. "Yes, I know. Of course, that's right. I'll take care of it," he muttered between her volleys of expletives.

At the top floor of the hotel, the elevator door opened onto the crowded hallway for our arrival, and she reverted to Hillary Clinton, the First Lady. I witnessed several incidents like this; and while I got used to Hillary's wrath, her ability to turn it on and off amazed me.

One time, though, her wrath was turned on me. It was on the president's trip to the Netherlands in May 1997. The president was commemorating the Marshall Plan at the foot of the architecturally stunning Erasmus Bridge in Rotterdam. The Dutch audience was wonderfully receptive. At the same time, back in America, a lady named Linda Finch was completing a seventy-three-day journey around the world flying a vintage Lockheed Elektra propeller-driven aircraft, emulating the failed attempt of Amelia Earhart. It was a journey that was being followed by the American press, but Finch's achievement was not even on the president's or the first lady's radar. They tended not to care about things that did not involve their own immediate interests. Thanks to a young enlisted military member sitting duty in the White House's Presidential Emergency Operations Center, however, we were tracking Linda Finch's progress. The young seaman called to notify me that Finch had arrived safely in Oakland. He would check on her availability for a potential presidential phone call. He kept me informed minute by minute.

I pulled the president and his personal aide aside and said, "Sir, Linda Finch has just completed an around-the-world flight, in Amelia Earhart fashion. She's now back in California with about thirty to forty-five minutes on the ground. Then she'll rest and head home to Texas. Would you like to make a phone call and congratulate her?"

He looked at me incredulously. "No, Buzz, not right now... maybe later."

The Clinton press office and staff had not been following the flight. It was the enlisted seaman who thought that he was making a useful contribution by suggesting the call. I thought he was right. But obviously it was the president's decision. Nevertheless, en route back to The Hague and the Noordeinde Palace, where we were staying, the staff discussed the possibility of a phone call during the motorcade over our secure White House Communications Agency radios. I told Kirk Hanlin, presidential trip director, that we were running out of time. "Kirk," I said, "Ms. Finch is going to get some rest and then fly back to her Texas home. We need to call now or not at all. She won't be available once she gets airborne."

Instead, the president and first lady decided to make an O.T.R. visit—an "off-the-record" visit—to the historic Dutch town of Delft. Delft is known for its porcelain dinnerware and rich history. Essentially, this little side trip superseded the phone call.

The unanticipated side trip to Delft turned a quaint Dutch town on a Friday night into a gridlocked security nightmare. At one point, the presidential motorcade was stuck on a narrow cobblestone street hemmed in by hundreds of people, many of them intoxicated and pounding their fists on the vehicles. As the scene grew uglier, I was genuinely concerned for the president's safety. Finally we managed, through the professionalism of the Secret Service, to untangle ourselves and depart safely. An hour or so later, we returned to our accommodations at the Royal Palace, the phone call to Finch seemingly forgotten.

It was one in the morning local time, and we were all ready to turn in. But then Mrs. Clinton approached me in the hall, just outside their suite, and asked, "Are we going to make that phone call, Buzz? Get her on the phone right now."

"No, ma'am," I answered. "I believe Ms. Finch is in an aircraft flying to Texas right now. We missed our window on this. The opportunity to call her passed hours ago."

"Why didn't I know about this?"

"I discussed it with President Clinton and the personal aide. We had an opportunity of about forty-five minutes to make the call, and we didn't make it. I'm sorry, but she is no longer accessible."

"Damn it, that's unacceptable! Why didn't I know about this? We can't miss opportunities like this. You get her on the phone!" she said, her voice raised and her face red. She spun toward Bruce Lindsey, who was standing nearby, clearly disappointed in me. "Bruce, you handle it," she demanded, and she walked away.

Lindsey turned to me and said, "You keep working that phone call. I'm going to bed."

Like hell, I thought, and I went to bed myself.

Linda Finch would miss her phone call. She was somewhere in the air—over Colorado, I was guessing. Vice President Gore would call her the next morning.

On a similar trip, as we lifted off a helicopter pad in Marine One en route to Air Force One for the journey home, Hillary suddenly shouted, "Put this back on the ground! I left my sunglasses in the limo." By this time, however, Marine One was safely scooting to an awaiting 747. The required support for even a helicopter flight was involved and extensive. The Secret Service, White House Communications Agency, and administration staff were pulling down communications lines, lifting barricades, and driving off in vehicles.

"Ma'am," my fellow military aide responded, "we can't safely do that."

"I need my sunglasses. We need to go back!"

The onboard Secret Service agent chimed in, "Yes, ma'am, the milaide is correct. That wouldn't be wise." She acquiesced, but not without obvious disdain in her eyes. Security be damned, those were her sunglasses!

Events and trips without her were akin to a frat house. It was hard to know which was better—the Nazi-like edge that emerged when she was around or the pseudo–Animal House atmosphere that emerged when she wasn't.

On Air Force One, the entire mood was altered by the absence of Hillary. The president felt free and acted like it. His whole demeanor changed. Even the menu for the flights was comically different. With Hillary, it was salads, low-fat dressing, and fruit plates. Without her, it was barbecue, Mexican food, and Philly cheese steaks.

The president had a swagger reserved for times like these. He told jokes and eyed attractive women. He sauntered down the aisle of the plane on takeoff and landing, when he should have been buckled in.

But when Hillary was with us, she ran the show. She was the power behind the throne, and her priorities came first. When the Clintons ran for president in 1992, they said they were giving the American people a two-for-one deal. What the American people might not have realized was that she was the more important part of the deal.

Of course, most of my travel was with the president, rather than the first lady. And it was equally disillusioning given what I assume most Americans consider acceptable behavior and acceptable priorities from American presidents.

Presidential scheduling for domestic White House travel seemed to me a cynical exercise. I noticed that most scheduled events were fundraisers for the Democratic National Committee (DNC) and not "official" presidential events. The president's schedule would typically include one or two "official" events and then at least as many, if not more, fundraisers or "political" events. And the "official" events, like school visits or labor union luncheons, were a transparent cover to make him available, at taxpayers' expense, to groups from whom he could raise the most cash for the DNC. A quick visit to an elementary school would be followed by a DNC luncheon, an expensive dinner party at a swanky hotel, and a late-night DNC-sponsored "Saxophone Club" event, where President Clinton would toot his sax and raise money with famous musicians like Michael Bolton, Art Garfunkel, or Tony Bennett. I could see Clinton's charisma pulling in the money.

But it appeared to me that something very important was being lost—namely, the president was spending more time raising money than governing the country. Even Clinton complained about the volume of fundraisers. "I can't think. I can't act. I can't do anything but go to fundraisers and shake hands," Clinton told his political advisor, Dick Morris. "You want me to issue executive orders; I can't focus on a thing except the next fundraiser."[2] Still, they went on and on.

There was nothing inherently "illegal" in this approach, but I wondered about the ethics involved. I wondered if the average American taxpayer would approve of Air Force One, Marine

One, the massive footprint of White House communications, and the salaries of the hundreds or thousands of traveling White House staffers being diverted to political use.

Improper use of taxpayer-funded support is one thing. But I was an unfortunate witness to the Clintons' taking fundraising to new lows when they rewarded big donors with nights at the White House or rides on Air Force One. I spent many nights on duty while the Clintons hosted donors and supporters. Visitors included politicians like Mayor Willie Brown of San Francisco and Governor Lawton Chiles of Florida, businesspeople like Harry and Linda Thomason, or Hollywood stars like Tom Hanks, Jane Fonda, and Richard Dreyfuss. Private showings of recently released movies were held in the White House Theater. Guests could bowl in the White House bowling alley. The ushers would provide fresh popcorn, and the guests would have an evening of informal entertainment followed by a night in the Lincoln Bedroom. The Clintons, as everyone would learn, were selling the sanctity of the White House.

But President Clinton somehow managed to convince the American people in the midst of every apparently politically deadly scandal that all was well, and that, if anything, he was the victim. That this was transparently false was clear to me from watching him.

His cynicism never ceased to astound me. In February 1998, for example, President Clinton and the staff decided to visit a tornado-ravaged area of Florida. We did an "I feel your pain" helicopter flight over and around the areas so that the president could survey the damage in which forty people were killed.

Colonel Ron Berube, the commander of the Marine One squadron and Presidential Marine One pilot, flew from one area of destruction to another, giving President Clinton and his senior staff a running commentary. He went to great lengths to plan the flight route and position the helicopter so that the president could get a real sense of the damage. The military aide had maps out to show the president just where they were and the extent of the devastation.

The president, however, was busy playing a game of hearts with his pals White House counsel Bruce Lindsey and press secretary Joe Lockhart. He couldn't be bothered—not even to look out the window occasionally. When it was time to align Marine One with the press helicopter for a picture, the president quickly peered out the window, feigning an interested and grief-stricken expression. The sole reason for the trip, in his mind apparently, was for that photograph. This playacting by the president was something I never ceased to marvel at—especially at how effective it was with his target audience. While he made a few mistakes—like walking in with a broad smile at Ron Brown's funeral—he almost always knew what to do to impress his audience. In that regard, he and the first lady were soul mates.

The behavior of the first lady and the cynical way the president approached his duties made my position difficult—at least to square with my conscience. But I reminded myself that I was an apolitical entity serving the office of the president—the office, not the man. That's how I approached each and every day at the White House. That's how I had to approach it, as the glow of that first Clinton handshake that had impressed me so much gave way to a more sober reflection on the president and his character.

In the military, spin doesn't very often triumph over substance, because the blunt edge of force—the reality of risk and potential casualties—cuts through spin pretty damn fast. But in the Clinton White House, the attitude was that spin could triumph over anything—and electorally for the Clintons, if not in the reality of foreign policy, it did.

And even when it came to foreign policy, President Clinton appeared to assume that the image of the well-traveled statesman would make up for a lack of actual foreign policy achievement. No president in our nation's history traveled more than Bill Clinton. In part, this was because he was trying to escape the scandals that followed him in Washington. But it was also because President Clinton was *intent* on leaving his own foreign policy legacy, just as every Democratic president had done since Franklin Delano Roosevelt. Defining that legacy, I saw, was a conundrum for him.[3] But the search for it took him around the world. President Clinton made 133 trips to seventy-four foreign nations or entities, a number never before approached by previous presidents. During his eight years as president, Clinton made more foreign visits than Presidents Eisenhower, Kennedy, Johnson, and Nixon combined. In his two terms, Clinton visited almost as many nations as Presidents Carter, Reagan, and George H. W. Bush combined.

Personally, I accompanied President Clinton on official state visits to the Philippines, Denmark, the Netherlands, Argentina, Germany, Bosnia-Herzegovina, Italy, and South Africa. For the

White House Travel and Advance staff, I visited Thailand and Australia, as well.

All of this from the president who, during the 1992 presidential campaign, criticized President George H. W. Bush for spending too much time overseas and not enough time on domestic matters. "It's time for us to have a president who cares more about Littleton, New Hampshire, than about Liechtenstein; more about Manchester than Micronesia," declared candidate Clinton.[4] In actuality, President George H. W. Bush never made it to Liechtenstein or Micronesia, but President Clinton did, visiting Micronesia when he visited Guam.

President Clinton's biggest travel year was 1998, the same year he was hit with the Monica Lewinsky scandal and impeachment. His foreign travel in 1998 accounts for one-fifth of his total travel over the eight years. Interestingly, President Richard Nixon's highest travel year was also the year he resigned the presidency.

Obviously, it is important for presidents to travel, as statesmen and world leaders. How much, though, should probably be answered by the taxpayers.

President Clinton's foreign travel cost the American taxpayers an estimated $500 million over his eight years. The figure is based on a National Taxpayers Union and General Accounting Office study of fifty-four trips.[5] This figure does not take into account Mrs. Clinton's or Vice President Al Gore's individual foreign travel. As first lady and vice president, they were authorized to use Air Force VIP aircraft, and they took advantage of it.

The first lady, for example, traveled to Africa, Portugal, Austria, the United Kingdom, Ireland, India, Russia, Panama, and

Canada in 1997. She visited Switzerland, France, Germany, South America, Bulgaria, the Czech Republic, and Central America in 1998. In 1999, she traveled to Jordan, Africa, Ireland, the United Kingdom, the Middle East, Greece, and Turkey. These were trips above and beyond those she took with her husband, and the costs in taxpayer dollars were estimated at about $12 million.

When she was campaigning for the Senate seat in New York, she routinely jetted up and back in an Air Force C-9A or C-20. The C-9A runs $3,366 an hour; the C-20, $3,587 an hour. As first lady, she made at least seventy solo trips to New York.[6] The real cost in terms of manpower and military capability to cover all of the Clintons' travel, foreign and domestic, may never be known.

The Clinton administration didn't just visit a foreign country; it invaded... and sometimes not so peacefully. When the president goes on a foreign trip, it involves an entourage that includes, at a minimum, staff from the Department of Defense, the Department of State, the Secret Service, and a number of other federal agencies, as well as an entourage of cooks, drivers, telephone operators, radio operators, speechwriters, stenographers, White House coordinators, facilitators, guests, members of Congress, and business and church leaders.

On my last trip with President Clinton, to Africa in 1998, one of the stated objectives was "to promote U.S. investment, trade, and economic growth." The accompanying staff totaled 1,302 federal officials. The Commerce, Treasury, and Trade Departments sent a total of eight people. The White House and U.S. Information Agency sent more than three hundred people.[7] Among the guests and staff were President Clinton's secretary,

Betty Currie, and the Reverend Jesse Jackson. Mrs. Clinton and Chelsea came along and spent most of their time sightseeing. There were more than nine hundred members of the U.S. armed forces along for support, enough to form an army battalion. We invaded, and I'm not sure the continent was ready for us. The sheer impact of the White House was almost comical. When I checked into our hotel in Johannesburg, the polite young lady behind the desk asked with a concerned look on her face, "When are you and your people leaving? There is too much commotion."

Air Force One is only one small piece of the logistical puzzle. In fact, most of the people and equipment necessary to support the president for a given location were carried by other U.S. military aircraft. For the Department of Defense, this means the massive airlift of people and equipment in advance of the president's actual trip by the Air Mobility Command, at Scott Air Force Base, Illinois.

The Air Mobility Command's primary mission is to move U.S. troops and equipment to battle, which, until my assignment to the White House, had been my mission. In the Department of Defense prioritization system, presidential trips and the associated support are coded "1A." What this means to the scheduler at the headquarters allocating the aircraft is that there is no other mission that takes priority. Not war, not common sense.

In real terms, whenever the president travels, soldiers and war-fighting equipment don't. For example, on Clinton's trip to Africa, the Air Mobility Command flew 144 cargo missions, transporting several hundred passengers and nearly 6.5 million pounds of equipment using primarily C-141 and C-5 heavy-transport aircraft. The Air Mobility Command flew an additional 110 aerial refueling missions using KC-10 and KC-135 airborne tankers. The Africa trip alone cost taxpayers at least $43 million.

On top of the cost in dollars, this trip to Africa caused the Air Force to cancel or refuse twenty-six missions and postpone thirty others. "The American taxpayer has no idea how many people get involved in these things," said one Air Force commander at Scott.[8] "It's excessive, and there's no accountability," another Air Force officer said.[9]

The president's trip to southern Asia in the spring of 2000, after I had left the White House, required 354 scheduled airlift missions. "This boondoggle will cost the Air Force over $50 million and limit its ability to execute its regular operational mission," an Air Force officer noted. These sorties "are enough to transport two Army divisions with all their stuff anywhere on Planet Earth," he added.[10]

In addition to directly supporting the globe-trotting of the Clintons, the Air Mobility Command was also forced to support domestic presidential junkets, and it took a huge toll on aircraft and aircrews, wearing out both machinery and personnel on missions of dubious importance. All of this at a time when the president was downsizing the military and compromising capability.

Virtually everywhere President Clinton traveled, he and his staff would insist on the availability of Marine One to move them from an airfield to another location, rather than rely on motorcades. Because Marine One was tasked with carrying not just the president and his immediate entourage but also additional staff and the press corps, it usually entailed at least four Marine helicopters.

The logistics of pre-positioning helicopters in cities across the globe are massive. In order to have Marine One and backup alert helicopters in Johannesburg, South Africa, for example, they have to be flown there. Not, however, as you would think. Helicopters are not capable of flying long distances over seas. The helicopters would have to be broken down by Marine maintenance crew chiefs, loaded into the back of the massive C-5, flown to the host city, often with several refuelings on the way, and reassembled by the Marine crew chiefs on the other end. The manpower expended is tremendous, and several days of dedicated support by the Marine Corps maintenance technicians would be required. The dollars spent were exorbitant. The cost to mission capability was devastating, particularly in a time of military downsizing.

For the Clinton administration trip to South America in October 1997, the Marine Corps had to supply the necessary helicopters to transport the press corps covering the president's arrival. "Showtime" was always an administration priority.

Of the many responsibilities that a military aide takes on when he works at the White House, the most demanding of his time is the travel, which involves advance work on the locations and detailed security plans developed in close coordination with the Secret Service—plans that make the military aide the quarterback in charge of moving the president and his staff safely away from any threat.

In my years in the Clinton White House, the military aides were also increasingly relied upon to take over the planning of

simple political events that were too complex for the many
young, inexperienced staffers that surrounded the president,
many of whom were hired as repayment for political favors or
campaign support, rather than for job-specific professional skills
and experience.

In late November 1996, a junior political staff member was
energetically planning an event for President Clinton's visit to the
Asian Pacific Economic Conference in Manila, the Philippines. I
was the military aide working most of the military logistical angles
for this highly visible, important three-day visit. The staffer was a
young Cecil B. DeMille type when it came to orchestrating events.
Nothing was too large, too outrageous, or too creative when it
came to putting the president's agenda across.

In an effort to arrange a fifteen- or twenty-minute photo opportunity with members of the U.S. Navy, the staffer requested
that the Pentagon divert one of the Navy's carrier battle groups
from off the coast of Australia into Manila Bay. "Then," he
explained, "we could helicopter the president out for a quick
'grin and grip' with the sailors on the flight deck. It would be
awesome."

Over several days, though, and through many phone calls to
Navy headquarters in Honolulu, we discussed the potential cost
in taxpayer dollars and otherwise. "You can't just move a carrier
battle group," I explained. "There are real-world implications. It
could be construed as 'saber rattling' or send diplomatic signals
that aren't intended. Plus, the cost in dollars would be stagger-
ing." I was finally able to convince him that whatever political
hay he might make through the resulting CNN sound bites

would be greatly outweighed by the cost in dollars and common sense. His dreams dashed, slump-shouldered and with a defeated look on his face, he agreed.

The Clinton staff could be publicly embarrassing as well. During the May 1997 presidential visit to Holland, our Dutch hosts rolled out the red carpet. Each Royal Palace room was stocked with food and a complete liquor bar for every staff member. A very thoughtful gesture, I thought, since we were getting in so late—a snack and a drink sounded great. The next morning, as we were leaving for Air Force One and our next country, the Dutch military aide pulled me aside to complain. "Your people took all of the liquor," he said under his breath, obviously embarrassed for me. "And they stole crystal and china, too," he added. He was completely floored by the audacity of the Americans from the White House. I apologized for the White House staff. But I'd seen it before. This presidency was all about *them*.

CHAPTER FOUR

FEAR AND LOATHING

They taught me that no man could be their leader except he who
ate the ranks' food, wore their clothes, lived level with them, and
yet appeared better in himself.

—T. E. LAWRENCE, *THE SEVEN PILLARS OF WISDOM*

ONE OF THE MILITARY AIDE'S DUTIES, when he accompanied the
president, was to oversee and control the passenger manifest for
Air Force One. There was room for sixty-eight people, the first
family included. The passengers on board were typically senior
White House staff whose presence could be easily identified and
justified, Secret Service agents, and a small press contingent.
Everybody's luggage, without exception, was screened by metal
detectors and bomb-sniffing dogs. Many times I'd be notified at
the last possible moment to add "presidential guests" to the
manifest. During 1995 and 1996, the Clintons invited at least
477 guests—excluding staff, family members, and press—
aboard Air Force One. At least fifty-six of these individuals had
donated $5,000 or more to the Democratic National Committee
or had raised at least $25,000 for the president's campaign.[1] I
knew that Air Force One was never intended for junkets or to
pay off favors.

Nor should it have been a sexual playground for the president—though even that took on an appearance of inevitability. In the fall of 1997, I received a phone call in my office from Lieutenant Colonel Mark Donnelly, presidential pilot and commander of the Presidential Pilot Office.

"Buzz, we have a problem," he said grimly. "One of my female stewards claims she was approached and touched inappropriately by President Clinton and she's upset."

I knew the woman Mark was referring to, and I liked her. She was bright, cheery, and beautiful. She was also an enlisted member of the United States Air Force—and had just, apparently, been sexually molested by the commander in chief.

"Where did this happen, Mark?"

"In one of the galleys on Air Force One on a recent trip. Apparently, he cornered her."

"Is she going to come forward? How does she want to handle it?"

"She's really upset but she doesn't want this to get out. She just wants an apology."

I said I'd talk to Kris Engskov, the president's personal aide.

I walked down to the Oval Office and found Kris. I pulled him aside and told him what Lieutenant Colonel Mark Donnelly had just told me. "I suggest, Kris, that you give Mark a call and arrange for a time where we can get the president to make a private apology." Kris agreed. I wanted out of this, and Engskov had a closer, more comfortable relationship with the president. He was, after all, one of the politically appointed insiders. I was an officer serving the presidency.

Two weeks later, Kris walked into the compartment where I was seated on Air Force One. He said quietly, "We got them together. The president apologized. She seems fine with it." I thanked him, and then confirmed his story in the cockpit with Lieutenant Colonel Donnelly.

I brooded over the fact that if our commander in chief had been actually serving in the armed services, he would have been jailed. His immunity struck me as completely unacceptable. Not for the first time did I feel that life was conducted in the military at a far higher moral level than it was in the Clinton White House.

Comparisons between the military and the Clinton White House were something that someone with my background made automatically. But even putting my background aside, surely the American people had a natural right to expect that the president and the administration would be cognizant of military and foreign affairs. Surely these subjects must be high on the list of priorities of any president.

But the Clinton administration's understanding of, and respect for, matters involving national security and things military just wasn't there. The sum total of its knowledge of the military seemed to come from movies and from the antiwar movement of the 1960s and 1970s. If a military matter didn't benefit Clinton and his people directly or serve to enhance their playing of domestic politics, it wasn't a problem for the president or most of the senior White House staff. Not only were they uninformed, but they were profoundly uninterested; they placed no value on what the military did. The military, in their view, was simply an administration lackey. In my opinion, no president in our history arrived in his position less prepared to be commander in chief than Bill Clinton. No commander in chief evoked so much outright and unexpected indignation from the ranks of the uniformed military than he did. And no president ever expressed such a callous disregard for the military as he did by deploying the military so recklessly, often while simultaneously seriously compromising military capability and degrading military morale.

Clinton was the first president in almost fifty years not to have served in the military. He is the only president to have dodged a Reserve Officer Training Corps commitment that he had made solely in order to maintain his "political viability." He was the only man elected president who could ever have written, as he did, "so many fine people have come to find themselves still loving their country but loathing the military." That combination of cynicism, of antimilitary loathing, of treating "a commitment to serve" as a mere scrap of paper to be abrogated by those clever enough, like himself, to protect themselves from "physical harm," were attitudes that he seemed to have brought from his past into the White House.[2]

Many presidents have lacked real, frontline military experience, and it has not affected their ability to lead our armed forces. President Ronald Reagan, for example, had no combat-arms military experience, yet he became, among the armed forces, one of the most popular and effective presidents. In part, this was because he had at least served in an Army military unit and reached the rank of captain working on home front celebrity activities during World War II. But even more important was the fact that he held the military in high esteem, made defense pol-

Flying into Grenada on the first day of the invasion.

On assignment as an operations officer at Travis Air Force Base, California, standing in front of a C-141...

...and in the cockpit.

Flying into Bosnia with Captain Chris Quiroz.

In Croatia with Senator Joe Biden and Senator Bob Dole shortly after our return from Sarajevo.

Official White House photo

Conducting business in the Oval Office.

Official White House photo

On board Air Force One. In case you're wondering, on the television screen over Clinton's left shoulder is "Dr. Evil" from the film *Austin Powers: International Man of Mystery*.

Official White House photo

Jogging with the president at Fort McNair.

Official White House photo

On the jogging detail with football in hand.

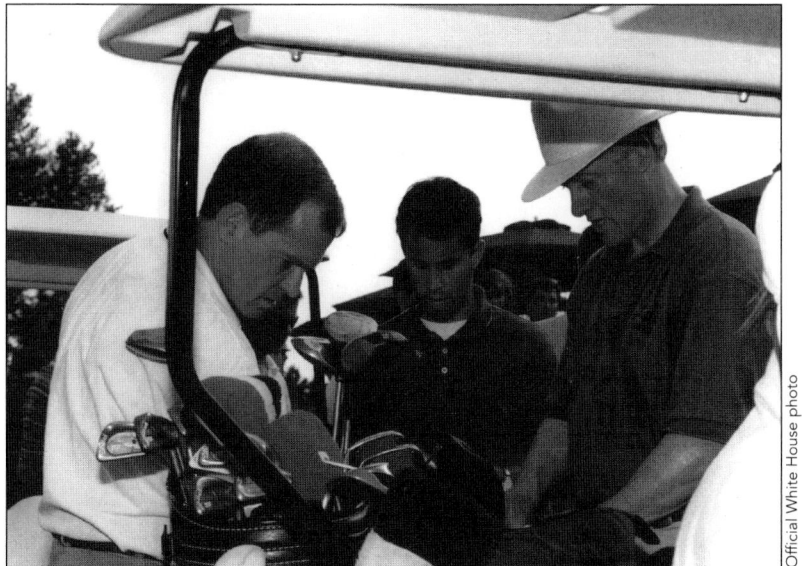

Official White House photo

On the golf course.

Official White House photo

My birthday on Air Force One. The president is playing cards with Doug Sosnick and Bruce Lindsey.

The military aide team when I first arrived. From left to right: Major Chuck Raderstorf, USMC; Lieutenant Commander June Ryan, USCG; Major Mike Mudd, USA; and Commander John Richardson, USN.

The president's birthday party in 1997. Presenting the gift of the military aides: jogging shoes.

Official White House photo

Performing a football skit for the president and Mrs. Clinton at his birthday party on the South Lawn.

Official White House photo

President Clinton awarding me the Defense Superior Service Medal at my Oval Office farewell.

Official White House photo

President Clinton presenting me with a symbolic football.

Official White House photo

The military aide team on my final day. From left to right: Major Duffy White, USMC; Lieutenant Commander Graham Stowe, USCG; Lieutenant Colonel Dana Pittard, USA; Lieutenant Commander Wes Huey, USN.

icy a high priority, and treated military personnel with obvious respect. Moreover, his cabinet for foreign policy and defense included Marine combat veteran George Shultz and Army combat veteran Caspar Weinberger. Clinton's high stepping through the Selective Service System in the late 1960s, coupled with his unwillingness to serve and "loathing" of those who did, was a different matter entirely.

One of the prime tenets of military leadership is that you can't ask (or order) someone to do something that you yourself are unwilling to do. Soldiers want to know that their commanders understand what it is like to be in the trenches, that their lives and the sacrifices they are making aren't being treated with disrespect or disregard. Credibility is absolutely essential, and the soldier, the sailor, and the airman can spot its absence immediately. Because Clinton loathed those who served, the understanding and respect he would eventually require from his troops would never be there.

The entire administration took its coloring from Clinton in this regard. The senior staff that led the administration when it was first elected had little to no frontline military experience. Vice President Al Gore served in the U.S. Army in Vietnam but did so from behind a typewriter as a public affairs specialist, safely away from the fray. Secretary of State Warren Christopher served in the Navy for three years during World War II in the Pacific theater. Budget director and eventual chief of staff Leon Panetta served in the Army for two years during Vietnam but did so as an attorney. Secretary of Defense Les Aspin served in the Army for two years during the 1960s but did so as a systems analyst. National Security Advisor Tony Lake and his deputy, Sandy Berger, had no experience in uniform. Lake, in fact, once resigned from the National Security Council in 1970 to protest the American bombing of the North Vietnamese. The experience of the others in defense and foreign affairs was even less.

The result was that no one in the White House really understood the people who risked their lives to serve their country. No one in the White House really understood the importance of esprit de corps or unit cohesion, or even how sending men and women into danger zones where the bullets fly needs to be done with a seriousness and sobriety of purpose that takes into account the risks and the costs. To the serving military, the foreign policy that emanated from the White House looked like gesture politics. The deployments we were ordered on never appeared to consider the well-being of those who conducted them. The White House never appeared to think it important that a military mission should be defined by an achievable goal that served our national interests. This basic understanding of military and defense policy, which any serving officer would understand, seemed to be completely foreign to the White House.

Worse, the White House's ignorance was compounded by arrogance.

During the administration's very first week, Army Lieutenant General Barry McCaffrey, the assistant to the chairman of the Joint Chiefs, greeted a young aide in a White House hallway. "Good morning."

"I don't talk to the military," the young aide replied.[3]

She may have thought she was being cute. But that story quickly circulated throughout the military and became the first of many blows that lowered morale and raised previously un-thinkable doubts in many military minds about the conduct of the administration.

The beat continued. The "gays in the military" issue was sprung on the armed forces—which had more important things to focus on, like defending the country—without any consulta-tion and by presidential edict. Just two months later, in March 1993, Secretary of Defense Les Aspin issued a memo to his staff directing that the number of military personnel in his office "be kept to the absolute minimum."[4] Another incident involved the French chief of staff, Admiral Jacques Lanxade, who wanted to meet with the administration regarding Bosnia-Herzegovina. Jen-none Walker, senior director for European policy on the National Security Council, told an intermediary that she wanted nothing to do with any French admiral.[5] Eventually, this undiplomatic incident was smoothed over by having the admiral meet with National Security Advisor Tony Lake.

And there were smaller things. President Clinton's early attempts at salutes to his Marine One and Air Force One crews, long a presidential tradition, were ill-conceived fingertip waves that made him look as if he were ashamed of offering a military salute. At events where the national anthem was played, he kept his arms dangling by his sides instead of resting his hand over his heart. The message, intended or not, came through loud and clear to the military: Bill Clinton and his administration knew nothing, and cared less, about the military.

Years later, my encounters with Vice President Gore were also telling. We didn't see much of the "VP" and his staff unless it was a campaign or fundraising event. On a few occasions, I found myself in uniform alone with Gore in an elevator or in a sequestered "hold" room.

"Good evening, Mr. Vice President," I'd offer formally. He'd look at me and look away. No response at all, at any time. Silence and the cold shoulder, that was it. The first time it happened, I wrote it off. The second and third times, I understood what kind of people we'd elected.

It wasn't just I or the other military aides or foreign officers or general military White House staff who were treated this way—so were members of the Joint Chiefs of Staff.

On several occasions I received phone calls from the office of General Ron Fogleman, the chief of staff of the Air Force. "Major Patterson, every time the general gets called over to the White House for a meeting, no one meets him, no one tells him where to go, where the meeting is being held; there's no protocol, no consideration."

Yet when Brad Pitt and Gwyneth Paltrow came to the White House for an event, you can bet they were met with bells on. I had to explain over and over to the Air Force that there was little I could do. If I was available, I'd happily escort the general. Normally, though, I was with the president or on the road, and the general was left to fend for himself. My fellow aides and I alerted the White House Social Office and the National Security Council that simple efficiency, let alone politeness or protocol, meant that Joint Chiefs of Staff ought to be met and escorted by an aide. They couldn't be bothered.

General Fogleman was a friend of my family's and the most respected Air Force chief of staff that I served under in my twenty years. Yet he retired from his position before his term was up because he "had simply lost respect and confidence in the leadership that [he] was supposed to be following."[6]

Early in the administration, the "buzz" was that Chelsea had refused to ride to school with her military driver and that Hillary had banned military uniforms in the White House. The president eventually called the uniform ban "an abject lie," once it became apparent that this story didn't play well politically.[7] I can't speak on whether Chelsea refused military drivers, but I do know the uniform issue with Mrs. Clinton was real. Soon after I arrived at the White House, my predecessor briefed me that Mrs. Clinton didn't want the military aides in uniform. The White House Military Office argued that, for the safety of the president, it was critical that the Secret Service and staff be able immediately to identify the military aide. Common sense and security finally prevailed—at least at official functions with the president. At all other times, however, we were expected to be in business suits or civilian clothes in order to downplay the military presence at the White House.

Sometimes even President Clinton, the glad-handing politician, let his contempt show. In spring 1998, a Marine crew chief on Marine One who had spent several years serving President Clinton wanted a photo with the president as a departing memento. He would be shipping off soon, and this would be his last duty in service directly to the president. This was a standard benefit for just about anyone who served President Clinton.

One of my fellow military aides pulled the president aside and asked him, "Mr. President, can we do a quick photo with the Marine crew chief? It's his last trip with you." The president glared at him. Undeterred, the military aide continued, "Sir, he's served you for four years and the picture will take twenty seconds. Could you please do it?" The president sneered, but acquiesced.

Once the picture was taken and Marine One was lifting off the ground, the military aide leaned over, caught President Clinton's eye, and thanked him. The president, obviously irritated, looked away and didn't say a word.

As commander in chief, President Clinton seemed to believe that he was privileged to conduct himself at a much lower code of conduct than the men and women he would repeatedly order into harm's way. At a time when his military was sending non-commissioned officers and senior military officers to prison for sexual misconduct, President Clinton was, notoriously, having his own personal behavior problems.

Many in the military lost complete faith and trust when President Clinton used the Soldiers' and Sailors' Relief Act of 1940 and invoked his position as commander in chief of the armed forces as a legal defense to delay the sexual misconduct suit of Paula Jones. The Soldiers' and Sailors' Relief Act was instituted to protect active-duty personnel from civil suits, such as divorce, until after leaving the military. Several veterans' groups protested and demanded that the president withdraw his argument. He did, thirteen days later, but only because it was legally untenable.

Events like this lowered morale, and the lowered morale developed into falling military performance standards and historically low levels of respect for the commander in chief. In one of President Clinton's first visits to a military unit of any sort, the sailors aboard the USS *Theodore Roosevelt* were openly derisive and disrespectful. Laughter and catcalls referring to Clinton's draft-dodging and his plan to repeal the ban on gays in the military echoed across the ship's deck as dumbfounded reporters looked on.

Air Force Major General Harold N. Campbell called the president a "dope-smoking," "skirt-chasing," "draft-dodging" commander in chief in a banquet speech. He was fined and forced to resign.[8] On several occasions, the separate services were forced to warn their members not to make insulting, rude, or disdainful comments about the president.

These highly visible incidents were only the symptoms, of course. Ultimately, in any military chain of command, the commander is responsible for establishing the guidelines for authority, morality, and capability. Clinton's primary downfall as commander in chief was his inability to bridge the gap between legal authority and moral authority. Legal authority resides in the president's constitutional rights as the commander in chief. Legal authority was his from the outset. But his moral authority was shot almost from the outset. A man who refused to serve when his country was at war was poorly placed to order other young men and women into harm's way. It was as simple as that at the start, but the administration took that poor starting point and made it progressively worse.

CHAPTER FIVE

NATIONAL DEFENSE OR SOCIAL PETRI DISH?

There are ways in which a ruler can bring misfortune upon his army:... by attempting to govern an army in the same way as he administers a kingdom, being ignorant of the conditions which obtain in an army.

—SUN TZU, *THE ART OF WAR*

MY LAST TRIP AS A MEMBER OF the Clinton administration was to accompany the president on his nine-day junket to six African nations in March 1998.

While visiting South Africa, I was riding in the "Control" van of the presidential motorcade along with Melanne Verveer, the first lady's chief of staff, and Bruce Lindsey. The motorcade was weaving its way from Johannesburg to the outlying township of Soweto and the Hector Peterson Memorial. President Clinton was scheduled to address the citizens of Soweto.

From the outskirts of Johannesburg, a clean, cosmopolitan city, we drove through miles and miles of shantytowns. The radio chatter between vehicles that normally occurs during motorcades was reduced to stunned silence by the extent of the poverty.

Ms. Verveer finally asked me, "How big is the South African military?"

"Ma'am, I believe it is the largest standing army on the continent, about ten thousand strong, I think, fairly effective and well equipped."

She paused and thought for a while. She then became visibly appalled. "Then why aren't they out here building housing, developing schools, road projects, things like that? They need to be helping these people." The other passengers in the van echoed her sentiments.

"Ma'am, I don't think that's the charter of their military, any military. In spite of the poverty and the obvious problems that we're seeing, I don't believe any country's national self-interests are served by using the military for public works. That's not why they exist, they're not trained for that, and they're certainly not equipped for it."

"Well, then they're wasting their money. They need to be doing something!"

And that, in a nutshell, was the Clinton administration attitude.

For the Clintons and their senior staff, the military was a social-service project. It had been transformed in a few short years from an instrument of national defense to an armed social-work agency. It existed for whatever ends this administration might have in mind. Certainly humanitarian relief, peacekeeping operations under the direction of the United Nations, and counternarcotics missions were accepted uses of the military by the Clinton administration. But it went far deeper than that.

A similar revelation had occurred months earlier for another military aide, U.S. Coast Guard Lieutenant Commander Graham Stowe. Graham was riding in a presidential motorcade in Rio de Janeiro in October 1997. Graham's van mates included Verveer, Deputy Chief of Staff John Podesta, and White House press secretary Joe Lockhart. As they wound through the squalor and poverty of Rio's slums, Melanne Verveer said that our military and Brazil's should be doing something about the terrible living conditions in Rio de Janeiro. Podesta and Lockhart agreed. Graham remarked to the Secret Service agent driving the vehicle that the military existed to inflict violence on the enemy— not to improve living conditions in Brazil. The agent laughed and nodded his head. That ended the conversation.

I mention these anecdotes because they reflect more than an antimilitary prejudice; they reflect what was a Clinton administration policy. While President Clinton was slashing the total active-duty force by about a third and increasing deployments by almost 300 percent, he also set out to reengineer the defense culture, which was historically geared toward fighting this nation's wars.[1] Under the Clinton administration, the military was to be refashioned as a tool that could be implemented for political gain, social engineering, and cultural experimentation. Issues such as "gays in the military," "women in combat," and the subordination of American troops to foreign commanders under the United Nations banner quickly became benchmark issues for President Clinton and his military.

Robert Bork, in his book *Slouching Towards Gomorrah,* calls the social agenda that liberals push at the expense of national security "radical individualism."[2] Liberal thinkers and revisionists like the Clintons are attracted to the military as a foundation for social change precisely because of the military hierarchical command structure. It is the very same reason that liberals are attracted to academia and to "reforming" the nation's churches. The hierarchy and authority of these institutions make them valuable targets for those who want to effect "social change." The case of the military is unique, however, because it is the one institution that liberals would like to seize and redirect without actually serving in it.

Lieutenant Commander Stowe told me that when he mentioned to a young lady who worked for the White House Advance Office, responsible for planning and executing presidential trips, that he'd received his undergraduate degree from the United States Coast Guard Academy, her jaw dropped.

"I didn't know that military officers had their degrees" was her response.

When she told him about her friends currently working on their master's degrees or going to law school, Graham mentioned that he, too, had a master's degree. In fact, he noted, all the president's military aides had advanced degrees. She couldn't believe it.

In the collective mind of the Clinton administration, a military career was unimaginable. As such, military men and women were of no consequence. More than that, as an institution, the military was putty to be manipulated.

Just one week into his presidency, Clinton tried to lift the fifty-year ban on homosexuals in the military. The original policy had been developed out of necessity during World War II. Congress had reaffirmed the World War II–era policies in 1982 when it declared that "homosexuality is incompatible with military service because it undermines discipline, good order, and morale."[3]

But on day three of his infant presidency, Clinton announced that he was ordering Defense Secretary Les Aspin to stop enforcing the ban on recruiting homosexuals and to halt prosecutions of homosexuals and that he would be signing an executive order removing the ban.

At the time, I was attending the Air Command and Staff College at Maxwell Air Force Base, Alabama. My class included some of the smartest officers I'd ever met. Our reaction was uniform: There'd been no debate, no discussion, no solicitation of ideas from the military; "Does anyone in Washington care what we think?" There could have been preinauguration meetings in Little Rock with senior military leaders to discuss the ramifications of such a radical change to military life. There could have been lobbying efforts and the soliciting of support from a very popular chairman of the Joint Chiefs, General Colin Powell. But there wasn't.

This policy would be water-cooler talk at every U.S. military facility in the world. Regardless of whether it was an issue of basic human rights or an issue of military readiness, the consensus among my peers was that the military was not, and should not be, the test tube for social change.

Fortunately for U.S. military capabilities and morale, and unfortunately for the political popularity of President Clinton, he didn't have the power to follow through on his promises. Just as he made a poor decision to pursue this issue so early in his presidency without consulting with senior military leadership, so too he made the mistake of not solidifying a congressional consensus prior to releasing the policy.

In particular, he ran headfirst into Georgia senator Sam Nunn, chairman of the Senate Armed Services Committee. Congress generally retains the power to make substantive changes to military policies and regulations. As a result, President Clinton declared that an "honorable compromise" was reached, and the infamous "don't ask, don't tell" policy was implemented.

On the heels of the gay issue, the administration pursued that of women in combat roles. The 1992 Presidential Commission on the Assignment of Women in the Armed Forces recommended by a vote of 10–0 to retain the Pentagon ban on women joining ground combat units, and voted 8–7 against female pilots flying combat missions. The commissioners who voted against women in integrated combat units were concerned about unit cohesion. They also cited studies showing women's shortcomings in upper-body strength and the natural tendency of men to protect women from physical threats. But the Clinton administration ignored these findings and moved to assign women to combat aircraft. The Navy, reeling from scandals involving sexual harassment in the service, aggressively implemented the new direction as a means to make amends. It also supported the repeal of the law exempting women from service on combatant ships, with the exception of submarines. The Air Force also aggressively implemented personnel policies to place female aviators into combat aircraft.

In 1994, Secretary of Defense Les Aspin opened hundreds of new positions to women in or near combat operations from which they had previously been excluded. The Pentagon's Defense Advisory Committee on Women in the Services, DACOWITS, a tax-funded defense feminist lobby, ignored the advice of experts and combat veterans and lobbied for the inclusion of women in direct combat roles, such as field artillery units and Special Operations helicopters. The irony is that during this same period, a poll of female soldiers found that only 11 percent of enlisted women in the Army would volunteer for combat. That 90 percent of enlisted women were self-described as not warrior material might be considered damning enough. To give women a combat role that neither they nor the military thought appropriate was an example of the administration's social engineering trumping reality—reality in this case being that the military exists for fighting wars. But combat effectiveness was not only *not* a priority of the Clinton administration, it did not even register on the administration's radar screen; and neither did the experience of other nations like Israel, Germany, and Russia, which now have stricter bans on women in combat roles than we do.[4]

The edicts by Aspin and the lobbying of DACOWITS led to the introduction of coed basic training. The Army introduced coed basic training in 1994 at its training facilities at Fort Jackson, South Carolina, and Fort Leonard Wood, Missouri. The Air Force and Navy quickly followed suit. Within two years, the military was rocked by sexual abuse scandals at basic-training centers at the Army's Aberdeen Proving Ground, Fort Jackson, Fort Leonard Wood, the Navy's Great Lakes Training Center, and

Lackland Air Force Base. The Marine Corps, on the other hand, enjoyed greater success in its training by housing and training male and female recruits separately.

The Marines were also the one service to oppose deploying females in combat roles. Assistant Secretary of the Army Sara Lister, a Clinton appointee, responded to this success by charging that the Marines were "extremists" and "dangerous" for not complying with the newfound need for integration of women into what were historically male roles. She also proceeded to make a joke about the Marine uniform.[5] Madeleine Morris, a Pentagon consultant on "gender" integration, suggested that the U.S. military should eliminate "masculinist attitudes," "assertiveness," "aggressiveness," "independence," "self-sufficiency," and "willingness to take risks."[6] She was serious!

God bless the Marines for standing by their tradition and not backing down under political and media pressure. America needs soldiers who are "dangerous" to the enemy, and we damn sure need soldiers who are "assertive, aggressive, and willing to take risks" when their lives and the safety of our country are at risk.

I've worked with and flown with female pilots and officers over my twenty-year career and can say without a doubt that they are as qualified and as professional as any man I've ever flown with. That women can fly as pilots is obvious. That unit cohesion and effectiveness is best served by putting women into combat roles is not so obvious; in fact, the evidence leans heavily in the opposite direction. But military readiness and effectiveness took a backseat in the Clinton administration to forced social engineering. Not a single military officer I've talked to doubts that women are every bit as capable as men in many military occupational specialties, but there are also significant costs to women's integration into many units, combat units in particular. Many officers, indeed, question the necessity of placing women on the front lines. The issues of forced sex integration, coed training, "dual" fitness standards, the need to redesign expensive equipment to make it coed, and the natural tensions and social awkwardness that these things bring with them are serious problems that lessen, rather than improve, the military's war-fighting ability.

The Navy's policy of "mixed-gender" crews on surface ships, such as aircraft carriers, has resulted in unexpected crew shortages, which debilitates combat readiness. For example, during 1994–95, on the first major war deployment of women aboard the carrier USS *Eisenhower,* 39 women did not deploy or were evacuated from the ship because of pregnancy. During the 1999–2000 deployment of the *Eisenhower,* 60 out of 492 female sailors—more than 10 percent—were nondeployable or evacuated from the ship, again because of pregnancy. On the USS *Roosevelt,* 45 out of 300 women—15 percent—could not deploy or were unable to complete the mission because of impending childbirth.[7] A Navy survey found that the overall evacuation rate for female sailors was at two and a half times the rate of men, primarily because of pregnancies.[8]

The Clinton administration attempted to cover up rather than deal with the shortcomings of its policy. Assistant Secretary of the Army Sara Lister told the press that the Army was reluctant to discuss physical-strength differences between men and women and pregnancy issues, because these subjects would be ammunition for conservatives seeking "to limit women's role in combat units."[9] In other words, reality and facts, in the administration's eyes, were inadmissible because they contradicted the administration's policy; reality and facts were ideologically biased in favor of conservatives! So it's no wonder that in the Alice in Wonderland looking-glass world of the Clinton administration, reality and facts were dismissed in order to cater to feminists and gays, other special interest group agendas, and liberal social dogmas.

While women and gays were welcomed into the military, veterans were handed their pink slips. When Vice President Al Gore was given the task of "reinventing government," he and the White House took credit for removing 305,000 people from the government payroll. What they didn't tell you was that 286,000 of those cuts—more than 90 percent—came from employees of the Department of Defense.[10]

During his command, President Clinton reduced the active-duty force by one-third to one-half, eliminating approximately 800,000 personnel. He reduced the Army from eighteen divisions to ten. He cut half of the Air Force combat fighter wings, chopping twelve from the existing twenty-four. He eliminated 232 strategic bombers and 2,000 Air Force and Navy combat aircraft. He reduced the Navy from 567 ships to just over 300. He eliminated thirteen ballistic submarines, four aircraft carriers, 121 surface combat ships and submarines, and most of the support bases, shipyards, and logistical assets needed to sustain these forces.[11]

He gutted military infrastructure and readiness capabilities, causing entire tactical air squadrons to ground half of their flights. He inflicted a dramatic decline in readiness ratings for ships in the Atlantic and Pacific Fleets. In late 1994, House Armed Services Committee chairman Floyd Spence issued an emergency fact-finding report stating, "Our forces are suffering through the early stages of a long-term systematic readiness problem that is not confined to any one quarter of a fiscal year or portion of the force.... The damaging effects of this readiness problem are being felt all year long, throughout the forces and in every service."[12]

The president also gutted morale. He immediately froze military pay at a time when it had already fallen behind the private sector by almost 20 percent. The pay freeze was especially egregious when approximately 80 percent of the force was earning less than $30,000 annually and more than twenty thousand enlisted personnel were eligible for food stamps.[13]

The Association of the U.S. Army coined a phrase, "the military poor," to describe the growing numbers of enlisted personnel throughout the Clinton presidency who were reduced to depending on food stamps and other forms of public assistance to support their families. Both the Army and the Marine Corps reported dangerously low reenlistment rates for their enlisted ranks, while overseas deployments were escalating. "Too many good, young Marines are leaving," said 1st Marine Expeditionary Force Sergeant Major Michael Magraw. "Many lance corporals and corporals are bailing out after their first hitch, because our operational commitments have been burning them out. And the pay they receive isn't enough to take care of their families."

A 1994 service-wide state-by-state study by *Parade* magazine of the U.S. Department of Agriculture's Women, Infants, and Children (WIC) supplemental food aid program found the number of enlisted military families living beneath the poverty line and using WIC services averaged between 12 and 20 percent of the total population of major military bases. Out of 5,400 sailors stationed at King's Bay, Georgia, there were 1,370 WIC families. Some 4,700 families were among 14,000 soldiers and Air Force members in the San Antonio, Texas, area. And out of 35,000 Marines in North Carolina, some 4,500 were WIC recipients.[14]

The true measure of the Clinton-Gore team and its views toward military men and women can be summed up in its actions during the presidential campaign of 2000. With the race down to the hotly disputed electoral votes in Florida, the Gore campaign attempted to disallow the votes of military personnel stationed overseas who had voted via absentee ballot. While the Democrats screamed disenfranchisement on the part of minority and elderly voters in Palm Beach, they were attempting to disenfranchise the men and women whose lives were on the line serving their country in a combat zone in the Middle East. The Gore campaign's lawyers asked the court to throw away the service members' votes, claiming the technicality that the absentee ballots needed postmarks.

That was sordid and unjust. But what was even worse was that President Clinton left his successor with an American foreign policy that was not adequately responding to the world's hornets' nests and with a military that was a shadow of the force that had won the Gulf War. And as with so many scandals of the Clinton administration, it wasn't Clinton, but our nation, that paid the price.

CHAPTER SIX

CNN DIPLOMACY

No one starts a war—or rather, no one in his senses ought to do so—without first being clear in his mind what he intends to achieve by that war and how he intends to conduct it.

—KARL VON CLAUSEWITZ, *ON WAR*

PRIOR TO MY ASSIGNMENT AT THE White House, I was an instrument of military force. Under President Clinton's command, I was called to support military operations in Somalia, Haiti, Rwanda, Bosnia, and Kosovo. As an officer and a pilot in the United States Air Force, I performed my duties to the best of my ability. While I did, I witnessed firsthand the withering effects of a commander in chief who orders his troops on superfluous missions with nebulous strategies and nonexistent military goals.

There's a quiet understanding when American men and women go into harm's way: We're in this together. There's also a deep trust that the government and military leadership that are sending them into action are doing so for the right reasons. Violate that trust, and there is uncertainty and doubt, which are bad things when bullets are fired in anger.

Over his two terms, President Clinton's decisions to deploy his armed forces mimicked the way a squirrel crosses the road—

darting halfway across, stopping and looking up into the head-lights, becoming confused, and finally returning whence it came.

From 1946 to 1991, the United States deployed military troops in eight foreign campaigns.[1] During the Clinton years, we deployed troops to at least forty separate foreign locations. The Clinton administration called these "unanticipated missions." My peers, fellow pilots, and aircrew members called them "channel surfing." Somalia, Rwanda, Haiti, Macedonia, Bosnia, Ecuador, East Timor, Kuwait, Liberia, Albania, Congo, Gabon, Sierra Leone, Afghanistan, Sudan, and Iraq were countries that saw direct U.S. military intervention of one sort or another.

We'd turn on CNN and look for our next assignment, our next conflict. The televised suffering of global conflict and eth-nic strife seemed to be the common denominator. But the prob-lem with television images, as a decision-making tool for military deployment, is that they can't accurately depict political com-plexities or military realities. And that superficiality was evident in the Clinton administration's deployment of our troops with-out any clear mission directives, with an unwillingness to apply appropriate amounts of force, and thus into the limited capabili-ties of "peacekeeping forces." When that wasn't sufficient, or was deemed inappropriate, the Clinton administration lobbed cruise missiles and employed isolated, ineffectual air strikes.

The results were ruinous, the specific engagements troubling. The Somalia debacle of 1993 was Clinton's first exercise in mili-tary deployment and the first case in point. Under Operation Restore Hope, then-president George Bush deployed 28,000 U.S. forces in late 1992 to provide and protect the distribution of food and medicine in war-torn Somalia.

I flew into the country in mid-1993, when our mission was still a humanitarian effort to feed and clothe the citizens of Mogadishu. It was a very pro-American, pro-UN environment. I never left the compound of the airport, but I could tell that everyone had a high expectation for mission success there. The next two or three times I went in, I noticed that we seemed to be stepping up the war-fighting aspect, taking in troops and equipment. The mission seemed to be evolving. We were not permitted to leave the compound of the airport because of the threat of hostile guerrillas in and around the airport. It was evident that the situation was sliding toward chaos. You could hear occasional rounds of gunfire and see the flames of burning buildings; you could see the Apache helicopters and gunships circling overhead. The degree of intensity was increasing dramatically.

The operation had grown into a nation-building commitment under Clinton. The critical juncture came in May 1993, when President Clinton declared the humanitarian mission accomplished. But rather than bringing our forces home, he left 4,500 American men and women in place as part of his vague policy of "assertive multilateralism."

The Clinton administration had developed a loose national strategy of "engagement and enlargement." In the eyes of President Clinton's national security team, foreign interventions would be primarily peace operations, and potential military involvement would be through international institutions like the United Nations. But in fact, this strategy left our forces undermanned and underequipped to meet the military reality on the ground.

On June 5, 1993, twenty-five Pakistani soldiers contributing to the UN effort were attacked and killed by Mohammed Farah

Aidid's militia. The Clinton administration had singled out Aidid as one of the chief barriers to peace in Somalia, and his attack on the Pakistani troops was the start of a war. UN bases came under mortar attack. Missiles were launched at U.S. helicopters. Snipers tried to pick off UN and American troops. Because the Clinton administration provided insufficient support, our forces had to depend on UN units. Our commanders weren't happy with the situation, nor that their request for armored vehicles and tanks to protect the troops, and other support, had been denied by Secretary of Defense Les Aspin. The Clinton administration insisted that "engagement and enlargement" were to be achieved while the military presence itself was shrunk. This was an obvious recipe for disaster, and the price America paid was the lives of eighteen American soldiers, the bodies of two desecrated and dragged through the streets. Seventy-three other soldiers were injured. Help was pinned down only a mile away—all because the request for armored vehicles and tanks had been denied.

As a postscript to the problems in Somalia, Secretary of Defense Aspin resigned. President Clinton announced he was sending in an additional 1,700 troops and 104 armored vehicles to "do the job right." That's when I got the call to fly in again.

I arrived in October 1993, a few weeks after the Black Hawk Down incident, flying a nonstop, twenty-four-hour mission from the West Coast of the United States. I brought my aircraft over the Indian Ocean and made a descent from the southeast into the airport at Mogadishu.

The water, crystal blue, was in stark contrast to the land, brown and barren. The sun was high and the air was filled with a smoky haze. A layer of dust hung in the air, haloing the city. There were intermittent fires dotting the backdrop. I banked the C-141 over the water, then over a tiny spit of land and onto the rough runway. The airport was a fortress. Concertina wire, UN troops in bunkers, rusting hulks of former Soviet MiG fighters, and blanched white concrete buildings surrounded the taxiways and tarmac.

After the tragic news of the previous few weeks, I was amazed and disturbed by what I saw. The war birds—the U.S. Air Force AC-130 gunships and the Army attack helicopters that normally would be patrolling the skies and suppressing threats— were parked and quiet. The troops were hunkered down. I expected our guys to be angry as hell and champing at the bit for some justice. But there was no energy; it had given way to malaise and resignation. "What in the hell happened here?" I thought.

The Black Hawk Down incident pissed off a lot of U.S. military people. The aircrews and the guys on the ground were ready to leave. Our original humanitarian mission had been an enormous success, but "engagement and enlargement" at mission's end was a disaster that served no purpose, had no definable end point, and was manifestly unachievable with the forces available. It was time to get out.

We off-loaded our aircraft full of support personnel, medical equipment, and supplies. Our next stop was Europe and some sleep.

In September 1994, we began our final pullout from Mogadishu and the UN operation in Somalia. In less than four years, the world's most powerful military force had come from the historic successes in the Persian Gulf to being beaten by a ragtag group of thugs in Somalia, and all because of an administration that had no real, definable idea of what it was doing there and none of the military and foreign policy expertise requisite to complete a mission of this complexity. More significant, an Arab extremist whose name few Americans had ever heard—Osama bin Laden—had achieved a victory, and his international al-Qaeda terrorists, who were fighting alongside Aidid's thugs, were emboldened to strike again.

An important sign of the Clinton administration's disregard for military and foreign policy is that there was never a "Clinton Doctrine" to replace the Powell Doctrine of the Bush administration, or the Reagan Doctrine, or the Truman Doctrine. All we had to explain our missions were variations on "engagement and enlargement." It became a common joke among soldiers, sailors, and airmen: "We're doing so much more with so much less that we should be able to do everything with nothing."

Realizing that Somalia had to be explained, President Clinton released Presidential Decision Directive 25 (PDD-25) in early May 1994. Essentially, PDD-25, otherwise known as Administration Policy on Reforming Multilateral Peace Operations, established specific criteria under which U.S. armed forces could be utilized in international peacekeeping operations. It seemed to be a complete reversal of the "aggressive multilateralism" the administration had initially espoused, saying that American armed forces would be deployed only when "American interests," "availability of troops and funds," "the necessity for U.S. participation," "congressional approval," and "a clear date for withdrawal" were established.[2] Nice words, but they were ignored. More notable, perhaps, but not receiving as much press, PDD-25 permitted U.S. forces to serve under foreign commanders. This tenet would come back to haunt us.

Nine months after I'd flown my last mission into Mogadishu, I made the long flight from the West Coast of the United States to the same region of the world. This time, it was war-torn Rwanda. Ethnic carnage and civil war had claimed an estimated 800,000 lives. It was early August 1994. There were 400,000 refugees massed at the borders.

This may have been the first time that U.S. forces were actually underneath a UN commander who was not an American. A Canadian general ran the show. The mission, strictly from our standpoint, was delivering security personnel, medical personnel, and supplies to the UN logistical operation that worked to save the refugees.

This being on the heels of Somalia, the administration made it very clear that the American involvement in Rwanda was "humanitarian support" and not "peacekeeping." In all, 2,300 American troops were dispatched, but to little useful purpose, and just two months later we were pulling out, having achieved next to nothing—nothing to stop the genocide, nothing really to justify our involvement at all. We never had the manpower, we never had the resolve.

At the same time we brought our forces out of Rwanda, we put them into Haiti. On September 15, 1994, President Clinton declared that "our mission in Haiti, as it was in Panama and Grenada, will be limited and specific."[3] Whether intentional or not, he made the speech on the very day that the last American troops were leaving Somalia.

The Clinton administration had already stumbled in Haiti once. In the same month as the tragedy in Mogadishu, the administration had sent the USS *Harlan County* to the docks of Port-au-Prince as a show of force. But an angry mob of Haitians was enough to force the U.S. Navy vessel to turn back. This time, with Operation Uphold Democracy, the Clinton administration deployed twenty thousand troops at an expense of at least $2 billion into the poorest country in our hemisphere—but again, without a coherent strategy. President Clinton's declared intent was to restore democracy in the form of elected president Jean-Bertrand Aristide and to rebuild a nation that was disintegrating. The undeclared intent was to stop the flow of thousands of Haitian immigrants who were making their way to America's shores. Ironically, Aristide, the man backed by the Clinton administration, was a committed socialist who had made a career of loathing the United States.

On September 19, 1994, the first U.S. troops entered Haiti. I sat in my squadron operations room at Travis Air Force Base, along with several squadron mates, and watched the "invasion" on CNN.

"Here we go again," complained one of my captains.

"I can't believe the president is putting us into Haiti...and for what?" echoed one of my staff sergeants.

The cynics said it was to score a "win" after the embarrassments of Somalia and Rwanda.

I flew into Port-au-Prince a week later. I carried in soldiers, jeeps, and communications equipment. The airport tarmac was loaded with American military equipment, personnel, and aircraft. There was so much military metal, the ramp was literally sinking into the bay. The disparity of this picture compared with the one I'd seen in Somalia was revealing and disappointing. When casualties were possible, as in Somalia, President Clinton used strong rhetoric and little action. When casualties were unlikely, he used overwhelming force.

The Clinton administration kept American troops deployed in Haiti for five years. We reinstated a leader in Aristide who maintained his anti-American rhetoric, allegedly restoring democracy in a nation that had never been democratic. We spent almost $3 billion in Haiti, but the Haitian economy only worsened, unemployment climbed above 70 percent, and drug trafficking increased. For the military men deployed there, these results did not lead to much job satisfaction or faith in the leadership of the Clinton administration.

Personally, I spent more time in the former Yugoslavia than in any of these other overseas conflicts. During the Bosnian war, before the Dayton Peace Accords, I commanded and flew the airlift of thousands of tons of food and humanitarian relief into embattled Sarajevo.

In June 1994, before I led my wing from Travis Air Force Base in California to Rhein-Main Air Base in Frankfurt, Germany—our first stop and our staging base for flying into the Bosnia-Herzegovina war zone—I called all the servicemen's wives and family members into our base auditorium. I explained to them just how serious and potentially hazardous our mission was. I promised to bring their husbands, boyfriends, and sons home safely—and I meant it.

My squadron wing, on very short notice, had been tasked to mobilize aircraft and crews to lead the resupply of food and medicine into besieged Sarajevo, Bosnia-Herzegovina. The war was still raging, the Dayton Peace Accords were months away, and the people of Sarajevo were starving. The Serbs had agreed to allow us to fly through a specific and narrow air corridor, then to land in Sarajevo. As part of the agreement we were required to land within five minutes of diplomatically cleared landing times.

We flew out of Frankfurt, Germany, five times a day, off-loading up to seventy thousand pounds of cargo—primarily food and medicine—and often many journalists.

We outfitted our aircraft with missile warning and other defense systems, lined our cockpits and seats with bulletproof Kevlar, wore helmets and flak vests, and outfitted ourselves with weapons. For many of my crews, it was their first time going into combat.

I flew our first mission into Sarajevo and the last one out. I wanted to set the tone. The flying was done in daylight only, as at night the airfield came under persistent mortar attack. The Serbs controlled the north, the Muslims controlled the south. The runway was the line of demarcation.

The first several missions were very eye-opening. Sarajevo is situated in a narrow valley. We would come in very steep and at high speeds to minimize our susceptibility to taking any kind of small-arms fire or antiaircraft fire. The beautiful landscape of green rolling hills studded with endless reddish-orange clay-tile rooftops was mesmerizing. Farmhouses damaged from repeated shelling, in various stages of battle decay, dotted the landscape immediately around the airfield. Battered apartment buildings, abandoned and empty, appeared to dangle like skeletons at the foot of the soaring mountains. Just ten years earlier this had been the world's playground for the Winter Olympics. The countryside was beautiful, the destruction complete.

On our approach into the airport, which had a small runway at a high field elevation, we often saw flashes from small arms–type weapons and heard the *thump, thump, thump* of mortar fire. From time to time, we took shots from snipers on rooftops. As we flew across the apartment buildings and onto the runway, we saw foxholes and pillboxes filled with United Nations troops—primarily French soldiers—who laid down small-arms fire in our defense.

Our rules of engagement were to land, off-load as much cargo and as many people as we could in a ten-minute window, and get airborne in the opposite direction. We did not shut down our engines. We did not remove our flak vests. We did not take off our helmets until safely out of harm's way.

We had a moderate capability to evade infrared guided missiles with flare dispensers. We never had a confirmed missile sighting, but the cockpit's audible warning tone alerted constantly, and the flares would fire. We were occasionally alerted by U.S. and NATO airborne command-and-control aircraft, AWACs, identifying potential threats.

In fact, on one mission, Captain Dave "Bubba" Guevera and I took Senators Bob Dole, Joseph Biden, and John Warner into Sarajevo as part of an early congressional fact-finding mission. As we were coming out of the Area of Operational Responsibility, my aircraft automatically launched flares to defeat whatever it sensed was about to happen to us. Senator Biden was in the jump seat between the pilots, and his eyes grew big as saucers. We made it out safely and into Split, Croatia. A few weeks later, some of our crews got shot up pretty badly.

When we first arrived in Europe, we were told to take off the American flags on our flight suits and to put on United Nations patches. We weren't very happy about that or about being told that we couldn't use American flight call signs. We reported to a British one-star general. The French ran Sarajevo, the Norwegians controlled Split, Croatia, and we did the large majority of the flying—which gave us the saving grace of returning to our American Air Force base in Germany every night.

For six weeks, we flew thousands of tons of food and medical supplies from Frankfurt into the tiny airstrip in Sarajevo with our lumbering, unarmed aircraft. Never before, or since, have I been so proud of a group of men and women, and so proud to be an American. We made our contributions to help feed, clothe, and heal the victims of a bitter conflict. I had my misgivings with our country's involvement in this arena, and with the command-and-control problems that were inevitable in a multilateral United Nations operation, but as a humanitarian initiative it was a worthwhile effort. I was also proud and gratified that every single member of my unit returned home safely, as I had promised their families before we left.

A few years later, I would return under peaceful conditions. I accompanied President Clinton when he visited Sarajevo and the U.S. troops in Tuzla, Bosnia-Herzegovina, in December 1997.

In the fall of 2000, I was again assigned to the Balkans as a member of the NATO occupying force. I was posted to NATO's Combined Air Operations Center for the Balkans, where my job was to coordinate the flights of all aircraft—military, commercial, and civilian—into and out of Bosnia, Croatia, Macedonia, and Kosovo, as well as to handle myriad other diplomatic and logistical issues.

I'd experienced the Balkans in the three distinct phases of the Clinton administration efforts. I saw the evolution, and I experienced firsthand the failed vision.

The fifteen missions I flew into Sarajevo, during my first deployment there as the commander of my deployed squadron, convinced me that the food, clothes, and medicine we delivered to the people of the besieged city should have been the extent of American involvement. Beyond providing humanitarian aid, we had no legitimate role in what was a regional war threatening no vital American interests. If there was backyard policing to be done, it seemed to me that that was the province of the members of the European Union.

Candidate Bill Clinton had made the Balkans a high-profile campaign issue in 1992. He had attacked President George Bush's lack of action in the Balkans. He campaigned on promises of lifting the arms embargo and of launching air strikes. But once elected and faced with the real complexities of the conflict, the Clinton administration fell into indecision. At one point, in a moment of complete frustration, President Clinton turned to one of my fellow military aides and asked, "Do *you* know what we should do in Bosnia?"

It was televised images of "ethnic cleansing" that prompted the Clinton administration to act. The massacres and atrocities became so outrageous that it started to hurt President Clinton's domestic political popularity. And so combined NATO air strikes on Serbian positions were launched and eventually led to the signing of the Dayton Peace Accords, on November 21, 1995. As a result of the peace agreement, however, President Clinton authorized the deployment of twenty thousand American troops as part of a United Nations peacekeeping mission. He promised that our troops would all be home by the following December.

Once again, the administration's decision to deploy troops ran counter to the stated policy in PDD-25. There were no intrinsic American national security interests in Bosnia. The requirement for a clear withdrawal date was met, or at least was announced, but that date would change, and then change again.

In December 1997, I traveled with President Clinton, the first lady, Chelsea, and a bipartisan congressional delegation into the Balkan theater. This trip was designed to visit the deployed American forces in Bosnia and build support for extending the stay for the NATO-led peacekeeping force. The plan was to fly Air Force One to Aviano Air Base, Italy, and change over to an Air Force C-17 aircraft for the flight into Sarajevo. The C-17s are similar in size to Boeing 747s like Air Force One but are more tactically equipped and have some defensive capabilities should there be a threat to the presidential party.

We departed Andrews Air Force Base en route to Europe in what turned out to be a thirty-six-hour day for me—one of the longest days of my life. Halfway across the Atlantic, I started checking the weather for arrival in Italy and discovered that it would preclude our landing. There were fog and severe visibility problems across most of Europe. I coordinated with the Air Force One pilot, Lieutenant Colonel Mark Donnelly, and we made the decision to divert to Ramstein Air Base in Germany.

The logistical coordination required for a diversion such as this was huge. The Secret Service agreed that Ramstein was a good alternative landing site. Via the satellite communications on board Air Force One, I called the Air Mobility Command Headquarters at Scott Air Force Base, Illinois, and I informed them that we were diverting and would they please alert the folks at Ramstein. I also called the C-17 aircrews waiting for us at Aviano and told them we couldn't get in. Fortunately, the C-17 mission commander was my White House predecessor, Lieutenant Colonel Darren McDew.

"Darren," I said, "we're heading to Ramstein. I know the weather is bad at Aviano but you've got to get your airplanes out of there and up to Ramstein."

Darren knew the implications. "We'll see you there," he said, with complete resolve.

In a matter of minutes, he had the crews of his three C-17s in the air and on the way to Ramstein, despite the horrible weather conditions. Three hours later, Air Force One touched down at Ramstein in blowing snow and high winds. It was three in the morning. As we taxied up the tarmac, I saw many uniformed military waiting to meet us. I didn't see the C-17s, however, and I started to worry about the house of cards we'd built. As the large 747 jet made the turn into our parking slot, I saw the first of three C-17s landing through the snow and darkness. We were right on the money!

The trip into Sarajevo and Tuzla, Bosnia-Herzegovina, was considered a success by the administration. The president met with Bosnian government leaders in Sarajevo and had a holiday meal with American troops in Tuzla. At one point, Mrs. Clinton pulled me aside and asked a curious question. "What do SFOR and IFOR stand for?" she asked as she pointed at some of the NATO troops and the patches they were wearing.

"Ma'am, they stand for Stabilization and Implementation Force," I replied. It struck me as odd that as engaged as she was in all of the administration's policies, she didn't understand the basis for the entirety of the United Nations and NATO mission in Bosnia.

We rejoined our Air Force One crews and aircraft at Aviano, where they had repositioned, and made the long flight back. In the early morning of Tuesday, approximately thirty-six hours after we'd left, we returned to the White House. In essence, this had been a public relations trip for President Clinton. Not in order to sell anyone on the NATO occupying mission in Bosnia per se, but to sell the "occupiers," the American men and women who would remain there for years to come.

Since the airspace over the former Yugoslavia remains "military airspace" to this day, NATO has the charter to control its access. During my last four-month assignment there at the headquarters for NATO's Combined Air Operations Center for the Balkans, I found the situation in some ways the same as it had been when I first arrived. Six years after I'd flown in humanitarian assistance, Sarajevo was still controlled by the French, Tuzla was still controlled by the Americans, and Kosovo was under an interesting combination of Russian, American, and British control.

On this assignment, I spent many days flying into the various airfields that years earlier had played key roles in the Balkan conflict, including Sarajevo, Tuzla, Zagreb, and Pristina. What I saw now was a peaceful occupation that will probably be required for years to come. I talked with many of my Serbian counterparts and asked them questions like, "When can you take back control of your airspace?" and "When will you be able to run your own air traffic control?" There were no answers, because they don't want the control back. Why should they? NATO is doing it for them. They've contracted out the management of their country, and at our expense. We're the caretakers, and the Bosnians are enjoying the fruits of our labors.

Somalia, Rwanda, Haiti, Bosnia: I participated in each of these engagements as an Air Force pilot and experienced the frustration of needlessly wasted lives, effort, and national prestige.

The military is a tool of national policy. It should be used to support and defend national security interests. Not all national security interests are equally important and not all require the use of the military. Effective use of the armed forces largely depends on an effective foreign policy doctrine.

The Clinton administration operated by the "CNN Doctrine." If it plays well on cable news, it'll be effective. Or so it was thought. The American military deployments in Somalia, Rwanda, Haiti, Bosnia, and elsewhere were largely reactions to perceived world crises that were not military crises that required American troops. But a president who had never served in the military himself never understood that, and never fully grasped or cared about the sacrifices made by our military men and women. Still, he exploited their patriotism and loyalty as they executed his orders.

CHAPTER SEVEN

THE WAR ON TERRORISM

War is an ugly thing, but not the ugliest of things: the decayed and degraded state of moral and patriotic feeling which thinks nothing worth a war is worse....

A man who has nothing which he cares about more than he does about his personal safety is a miserable creature who has no chance of being free, unless made and kept so by the existing of better men than himself.

—JOHN STUART MILL

"THE CONTEST IN AMERICA"

DISSERTATIONS AND DISCUSSIONS

THE WHITE HOUSE SITUATION ROOM was buzzing. It was fall 1998 and the National Security Council (NSC) and the "intelligence community" were tracking the whereabouts of Osama bin Laden, the shadowy mastermind of terrorist attacks on American targets overseas. "They've successfully triangulated his location," yelled a "Sit Room" watch stander. "We've got him."

Beneath the West Wing of the White House, behind a vaulted steel door, the Sit Room staff sprang into action. The watch officer notified National Security Advisor Sandy Berger, "Sir, we've located bin Laden. We have a two-hour window to strike."

Characteristic of the Clinton administration, the weapons of choice would be Tomahawk missiles. No clandestine "snatch" by our Special Operations Forces. No penetrating bombers or high-speed fighter aircraft flown by our Air Force and Navy forces. No risk of losing American lives.

Berger ambled down the stairwell and entered the Sit Room. He picked up the phone at one of the busy controller consoles and called the president. Amazingly, President Clinton was not available. Berger tried again and again. Bin Laden was within striking distance. The window of opportunity was closing fast. The plan of attack was set and the Tomahawk crews were ready. For about an hour Berger couldn't get the commander in chief on the line. Though the president was always accompanied by military aides and the Secret Service, he was somehow unavailable. Berger stalked the Sit Room, anxious and impatient.

Finally, the president accepted Berger's call. There was discussion, there were pauses—and no decision. The president wanted to talk with his secretaries of defense and state. He wanted to study the issue further. Berger was forced to wait. The clock was ticking. The president eventually called back. He was still indecisive. He wanted more discussion. Berger alternated between phone calls and watching the clock.

The NSC watch officer was convinced we had the right target. The intelligence sources were conclusive. The president, however, wanted a guaranteed hit or nothing at all.

This time, it was nothing at all. We didn't pull the trigger. We "studied" the issue until it was too late—the window of opportunity closed. Al-Qaeda's spiritual and organizational leader slipped through the noose.

This lost bin Laden hit typified the Clinton administration's ambivalent, indecisive way of dealing with terrorism. Ideologically, the Clinton administration was committed to the idea that most terrorists were misunderstood, had legitimate grievances, and could be appeased, which is why such military action as the administration authorized was so halfhearted, and ineffective, and designed more for "show" than for honestly eliminating a threat.

When on February 26, 1993, Egyptian and Palestinian terrorists blew a hole six stories deep under the North Tower of the World Trade Center, President Clinton had been in office thirty-eight days. Eight months after President Clinton left office, al-Qaeda terrorists flew hijacked U.S. commercial airliners into the North and South Towers of the World Trade Center and into the Pentagon. The towers came down, as the terrorists finished the job begun eight years earlier. From 1993 to 2001, Islamic terrorists attacked American targets eight separate times. If there's anything beyond scandal that we should most remember about the Clinton years, this is it: They were the years that terrorists brought their war to the United States.

The Clinton administration never responded decisively, even when given the opportunity, as it was obliged to do, with its own "war against terrorism." If we had a national interest in sending troops to Haiti and Rwanda, certainly the Clinton administration had an obligation in the name of our national security to deploy and use the military resources necessary to deal with al-Qaeda as its deadly presence became known and its declared war on America became public and costly. That it did not respond is a consequence for which the Clinton administration is, in my view, extremely culpable. By failing to answer the threat as it should have, the Clinton administration was guilty of gross negligence and dereliction of duty to the safety of our country, which the president was sworn to defend.

Compare this with the decisive reactions to fight terrorism under President Reagan. On October 8, 1985, a group of Palestinian terrorists seized the Italian luxury liner *Achille Lauro* off the coast of Alexandria, Egypt. The terrorists were seeking the release of Palestinian prisoners being held by Israel. In the course of their hijacking, they would kill an American, sixty-nine-year-old Leon Klinghoffer.

The direction from the White House down to the Pentagon and on to the operational units was swift and clear. Within a few hours, I received a phone call at home, quickly packed for an unknown period of time and destination, and was flying a C-141 from Charleston Air Force Base, South Carolina, to pick up members of the First Special Forces Operational Detachment–Delta, as it was known then, or Delta Force.

We flew nonstop to Sigonella Naval Air Station in Sicily and set up operations for the potential interdiction and seizure of the ship. The rapidity and strength of executive decision-making found refuge in the heart of every airman and soldier involved. There was no question as to our intent or conviction.

The terrorists left the boat under safe haven provided by Egypt two days later and boarded an Egyptian airliner bound for the sanctity of Tunisia. On October 11, U. S. Navy F-14 jets intercepted the airliner and forced it to land at Sigonella. Members of the Delta Forced poured from a following C-141, surrounded the jet, and quickly took the terrorists into captivity. In all, three days from presidential directive to successful outcome.

In another instance, the La Belle Discotheque in West Berlin was bombed on April 5, 1986, killing one American soldier and wounding more than two hundred, of which at least sixty were fellow U.S. servicemen. Within hours, the U.S. pinpointed Libya as the perpetrator through intercepted telephone calls. Two days later, my crew and I got the call and began the long flight east. This time we were hauling the armaments, the missiles, and the rocket motors to be installed on U.S. fighters at bases in the United Kingdom. When we arrived, we were met by an already established twenty-four-hour base of operations. Again it was clear: Here was conviction and resolve. The plans were being laid out, and every airman knew the situation and embraced it.

On April 15, the U.S. launched air strikes at the heart of Libya. Eighteen U.S. Air Force F-111 aircraft attacked sites in Tripoli, firing missiles at military barracks, headquarters, the Tripoli airport, and commando training bases. Fifteen U.S. Navy A-6 and A-7 attack jets hit military targets in Benghazi.

President Reagan addressed the nation. "Our evidence is direct, it is precise, and it is irrefutable. Today we have done what we had to do. If necessary, we shall do it again....He [Muammar Qaddafi] counted on America to be passive," declared the president. "He counted wrong."[1]

Compare these successes with the legacy of the Clinton administration. The truck bomb that exploded beneath the World

Trade Center in early 1993 killed six Americans and injured more than one thousand. Initially, the Clinton administration adopted the theory that it was a simple criminal act and handled the bombing as a law enforcement issue. President Clinton even warned Americans against "overreacting." In an interview with MTV he described the attack as having been perpetrated by someone who "did something really stupid."[2] In no way did the administration see this terrorist attack as rivaling in importance its preferred issues of "it's the economy, stupid," socializing health care, and lifting the ban on homosexuals in the military.

Treating the bombing solely as a law enforcement issue created barriers preventing an effective resolution. Laws protecting grand jury secrecy neutralized the involvement of the intelligence agencies, in effect obstructing the identification and pursuit of a growing international terror network. Further complicating things, the administration's law enforcement team was not yet in place, because of the ill-organized and scandal-ridden selection process of President Clinton's cabinet.

Foreboding clues emerged throughout the World Trade Center investigation, pointing to a larger, more complex conspiracy. Testifying to the House International Relations Committee in April 1995, terrorism expert Steven Emerson stated that there was evidence "pointing to the involvement of Usama bin Laden, the ex-Afghan Saudi Mujahideen supporter now taking refuge in the Sudan."[3]

Sheikh Omar Abdel-Rahman, who'd held three U.S. visas and was also on the State Department's watch list for his involvement in the assassination of Egypt's Anwar Sadat, was eventually convicted and sentenced to life imprisonment as the ringleader of the bombing. The same fate was handed down to five of his associates.

More important, an ancestral tree of terrorism was emerging. Ramzi Ahmed Yousef, a master bomb builder, was captured in Pakistan on February 7, 1995. He was implicated in the first World Trade Center bombing and accused of planting the bomb that exploded aboard a Filipino commercial airliner en route to Japan in 1995. He was arrested with files connecting him to al-Qaeda and financing through bin Laden's brother-in-law. Most significant, he was suspected of developing plans to use commercial airliners as weapons, specifically to blow up the Central Intelligence Agency headquarters in Langley, Virginia, among other targets. Filipino intelligence sources had intercepted terrorist plans, which the terrorists had code-named Operation Bojinka, or "loud bang" in Serbo-Croatian. But this developing picture was not welcomed by the Clinton administration, which took a heavily lawyerly approach—as suited the backgrounds of most of the administration—toward these developments, rather than an approach more suitable to our national security.

The single event that would forever underscore Clinton's foreign policy efforts occurred on October 3, 1993—the Black Hawk Down incident that pitted American forces against warlord Mohammed Farah Aidid, the emerging power behind the guerrilla warfare being fought in and around Mogadishu. The Black Hawk Down military failure shaped and reinforced the president's unfocused posturing involving military action abroad; his preferred means of operation was showing the flag while not incurring the risk or the cost of having to support actual combat. Clinton's response four days after Mogadishu was to announce the withdrawal of American combat troops and most logistics units. He declared that the U.S. role in Somalia would end by March 31, 1994.

This was true, even when, in November 1996, bin Laden confessed in an interview with the London-based *Al-Quds Al-Arabi* newspaper to his role in the heavy losses suffered by U.S. troops in Somalia. "The only non-Somali group which fought the Americans are the Arab Mujahedeen who were in Afghanistan," he said. "There were successful battles in which we inflicted heavy losses against the Americans. We used to hunt them in Mogadishu."[4]

On March 8, 1995, a seemingly minor news account provided additional clues. Two U.S. consulate workers were killed in Karachi, Pakistan. Their van, with diplomatic license plates, was sprayed with bullets from men armed with AK-47 assault rifles. Speculation pointed to retaliation for the arrest and extradition of Ramzi Yousef. Pakistani prime minister Benazir Bhutto called it "part of a well-planned campaign of terrorism." President Clinton called the attack a "cowardly act" and sent an FBI team to Pakistan to investigate.[5] Again, the administration chose to treat the latest act of terrorism as a law enforcement issue.

By 1995, the administration was paying close attention to bin Laden. He was a millionaire, associated with known terrorist groups, and he had openly detailed his hostility toward the United States. At this point, bin Laden had yet to be tied to the attacks at the World Trade Center or in Mogadishu. The government of Sudan, in an effort to improve its diplomatic standing with America, offered to turn the terrorist-supporting bin Laden over to the Saudis, but the Saudis refused to accept him, and President Clinton felt that U.S. legal action against bin Laden was as yet unwarranted.

In November 1995, a bomb exploded near a U.S. military training center in the Saudi Arabian capital of Riyadh. Seven people were killed, including five Americans, and forty were wounded. It was the deadliest such attack since the Beirut bombings of 1983.

President Clinton reacted angrily to the news. He promised that the United States would "devote an enormous effort" to bringing the attackers to justice. The FBI sent a team of agents to investigate, but the agents soon became bogged down in Saudi bureaucracy. The Saudis eventually arrested four militants but beheaded them before the FBI could interrogate them.

Seven months after the bombing in Riyadh, on June 25, 1996, a truck bomb exploded outside Khobar Towers, the U.S. Air Force barracks in Dhahran, Saudi Arabia. Nineteen airmen lost their lives and 515 were wounded. "The explosion appears to be the work of terrorists, and if that is the case, like all Americans, I am outraged by it," President Clinton declared. "We will pursue this.... America takes care of our own. The cowards who committed this murderous act must not go unpunished."[6]

One month into my White House job, on June 30, 1996, I traveled with President Clinton to Eglin Air Force Base, Florida, to attend one of the memorial services held in a large aircraft hangar for twelve of the slain airmen. It was a hot, muggy Florida morning, and on the way to the service President Clinton seemed strangely detached. Maybe it was the jet-lagging flight back from Europe that he'd just had. To me, he just seemed unaffected and unmoved.

We wound our way through the crowded hangar normally used for aircraft maintenance but now festooned with stars-and-stripes bunting. Injured survivors from the blast had been flown in from the Gulf. They sat in wheelchairs or were laid on gurneys in front of the stage. President Clinton stepped to the podium. In the spotlight, he suddenly became engaged and driven.

He invoked the Bible in a way that touched me as a career Air Force officer and as a Christian. He said, "There is a passage in Isaiah in which God wonders, 'Whom shall I send, and who will go for us?' Isaiah answers, 'Here I am Lord; send me.' These men we honor today said to America, 'Send me.'" Clinton then declared, "We will not rest in our efforts to capture, prosecute, and punish those who committed this evil deed.... America must not, and America will not, be driven from the fight against terrorism."[7] I believed him.

But there was no immediate response. The FBI concluded that Iran was behind the attack; administration officials suppressed the report. In pursuit of secret diplomatic initiatives to restore ties with Iran that would ultimately fail, the United States turned the other cheek.

A full five years later, on June 21, 2001, a federal grand jury in Washington indicted thirteen Saudis and a Lebanese for taking part in the attack. None were turned over to the United States, and extradition still appears unlikely.

During the summer of the 1996 attacks, I myself learned first-hand that the administration knew that terrorists were plotting to use commercial airliners as weapons. The president received a Presidential Daily Brief, or PDB, every morning. It was a document encased in a smart leather folder, and emblazoned with the presidential seal, that contained the president's daily intelligence update from the NSC. A senior NSC representative normally delivered it to the president. On weekends, at Camp David, and on vacations, the military aide was responsible for delivering and retrieving the brief.

One late-summer Saturday morning, the president asked me to pick up a few days' worth of PDBs that had accumulated in the Oval Office. He gave them to me with handwritten notes stuffed inside the folders and asked that I deliver them back to the NSC.

I opened the PDB to rearrange the notes and noticed the heading "Operation Bojinka." I keyed on a reference to a plot to use commercial airliners as weapons and another plot to put bombs on U.S. airliners. Because I was a pilot, this naturally grabbed my attention. I can state for a fact that this information was circulated within the U.S. intelligence community, and that in late 1996 the president was aware of it.

Shortly thereafter, the president appointed Vice President Gore to chair the White House Commission on Aviation Safety and Security. The commission's report, released in spring 1998, laid out several recommendations to improve airport security, one of which included establishing a system for profiling passengers. But the FAA chose not to comply, because of inevitable fears that profiling on the basis of ethnicity and national origin would run into legal grounds that would violate civil liberties. Another recommendation from the report emphasized the need for interagency cooperation—specifically, the sharing of information among the Central Intelligence Agency, the Federal Bureau of Investigation, the Immigration and Naturalization Service, and the Federal Aviation Administration—on suspected terrorists. Tragically, the findings were never implemented by the agencies involved.

On August 7, 1998, truck bombs exploded at the U.S. embassies in Nairobi, Kenya, and Dar es Salaam, Tanzania. Two hundred and twenty-four people were killed, twelve of them Americans. More than five thousand were injured. President Clinton responded, "We will use all the means at our disposal to bring those responsible to justice, no matter what or how long it takes.... We are determined to get answers and justice."[8]

It was crystal clear that these attacks were tied to bin Laden. On August 20, the president ordered a retaliatory strike. Five U.S. warships in the Arabian Sea fired sixty Tomahawk cruise missiles at four suspected terrorist camps in Afghanistan known to be used by bin Laden and his senior staff. From the Red Sea, two Navy warships fired another twenty missiles at the Al-Shifa pharmaceutical plant, in Sudan, suspected of manufacturing chemical weapons.

The attack on bin Laden failed. He escaped the missiles and was able to enjoy his safety as a guest of Afghanistan's Taliban government. The success of the attack on the pharmaceutical factory was less clear. Intelligence officials had provided evidence that the plant could have been used for the development of VX nerve gas. At best, the strikes were a message; at worst, they were ineffective and insignificant.

In the wake of the retaliatory strikes, Secretary of State Madeleine Albright noted, "I think it's important for the American people to understand that we are involved in a long-term struggle. This is, unfortunately, the war of the future."[9] But it was obvious to me that the Clinton administration went right back to business as usual; there was no follow-up, let alone any "war on terror."

Two years later, on October 12, 2000, the final act of terrorism during the Clinton presidency occurred. Seventeen American sailors were killed and thirty-nine wounded off the coast of Yemen when terrorists floated a bomb-laden boat to the edge of the USS *Cole* and detonated it. Clinton's response was muted. He called the attack "a despicable and cowardly act" and added, "We will find out who was responsible and hold them accountable."[10] As in the embassy bombings, investigators quickly linked responsibility to bin Laden and his network, yet nothing more substantial was done.

In his eight years in office, President Clinton's military response to the terrorist threats was negligible and did nothing to seriously address the problem, instead following a de facto course of drift, which allowed the terrorist network to grow in size and strength. The problem within the administration was, again, a complete and total blindness to the proper use of the military. Terrorism was, as I've said, treated as a law enforcement issue, and in that context, as a budgetary issue, it *was* addressed.

President Clinton tripled the budget for counterterrorism and established a cross-agency counterterrorism center. Terrorism "was absolutely a top priority for the Clinton administration. Not a day went by that we did not focus on this, and it was high on the president's list, too," claimed former national security advisor Sandy Berger.[11] Maybe, but President Clinton never began, much less finished, a war on terrorism, because he never thought in terms of prosecuting a military campaign against terrorism, and he underestimated the rapidly evolving threat until it was too late.[12]

As ever with President Clinton, it was domestic politics that "wagged the dog." He did not want a war against terrorism as a focal point in his new administration, so he downplayed the first World Trade Center bombing. Later, the focal points were re-election or scandal management. Never in my experience at the Clinton White House were national security and a systematic campaign against terrorism a Clinton administration priority. And as an officer, I was shocked, because I had assumed that there was not a higher responsibility or priority for the commander in chief than the security of the nation. President Clinton proved my assumption was completely wrong.

Chapter Eight

A Time to Move On

Leadership involves conduct. Conduct is determined by values.
Values are what makes us who we are.

—General H. Norman Schwarzkopf

October 30, 1997

In the spring of 1998, the exuberance and energy of the White House staff that had initially amazed me when I arrived in Washington just two years earlier had deteriorated into foreboding and a sense of defeat. The battering the administration was taking from the endless revelations of scandal had deflated the White House staffers' morale; those who once vigorously defended the president now had little or nothing to say.

The military aides, while officially apolitical, felt just as tarnished by the shame and embarrassment that was overwhelming the White House staff. We discussed the stigma that would be attached to each of us when we returned to our services. One of the aides refused his official Oval Office farewell from the president. Another aide was concerned about the negative repercussions from having the president's name and signature on his annual evaluation report. Collectively, we were all concerned about returning to our respective services into positions of command and having to lead young men and women who knew that our résumés included serving as an aide to President Clinton; we feared it would besmirch us as being "political" officers rather than sincere, trustworthy, committed, and moral leaders of warriors.

At one time or another, we all wanted out. At one point, we even discussed resigning en masse. The symbolic nature of the five military aides leaving our positions simultaneously in disgust was something we contemplated and seriously considered. We recalled the Joint Chiefs during Vietnam and their failure to take a principled stand. Now, although much more junior in rank, we too had an opportunity to do the right thing. We had been carefully selected for this assignment, we were capably representing our individual services, and we strove to professionally represent the calling of military officership. We were also very conscious of the fact that we represented all the previous military aides who had served their presidents with honor and distinction.

Ultimately, we came to the consensus that we were serving the office and our country, not the man who held the presidency. Still, in the months leading up to my departure, I had become completely dejected. As my final days approached, I couldn't wait to leave. The Air Force, thank goodness, helped me to find my way forward. General Walter Kross, commander of the Air Mobility Command, my Air Force "home" command, personally called and asked me what I wanted to do and where I wanted to go next. I respected him immensely as a leader and a gentleman. I'd had the opportunity to serve under him while I was stationed at Travis Air Force Base, and I knew him as one of the "good guys" that the Air Force had in senior leadership positions. He was supporting me for command of a flying squadron.

"Sir," I offered, "I need to fly out and see you. I've got some things on my mind that may not be in line with your expectations. I need to discuss them with you personally." He agreed, and I flew out to Illinois a few weeks later to meet with him.

We sat down in his office at Scott Air Force Base and talked about my future. I told him that my career goals and personal aspirations had changed. My time at the White House had been difficult—not only for myself, but because I was recently married, and continual travel was not conducive to the sort of home life I wanted to have. Instead of assuming command of a flying squadron, I wanted to go back to the roots, back to the origins of officership, integrity, and honor. It was a tough thing for me to say, because commanding a squadron was something I knew how to do, and I felt competent and honored to lead the young men and women of an Air Force squadron. But I had made my decision: I wanted to be reassigned to the United States Air Force Academy, a completely new and unfamiliar challenge, but one that I felt would be a great relief from my time in the Clinton White House.

With the many assignment opportunities available to me and all the avenues that the Air Force was making available to me, serving at the Air Force Academy made the most sense. It was important to me to reclaim my pride, my self-respect, and I decided the best way to accomplish that would be by teaching future officer candidates the meaning of honor, integrity, and character. I wanted a return to the naïveté and innocence of college-aged men and women just starting out in their pursuit of the profession of arms. I wanted to wake up each morning and, as General Fogleman so aptly put it when he retired, ask myself, "Do I feel honorable and clean?" and be able to answer yes.

General Kross understood my wishes, and though he wanted me to accept the squadron command, he agreed to arrange for me to take a position at the Air Force Academy. In a few short months, I would take command of an Air Force Academy group of one thousand cadets and future officer candidates as Cadet Group Commander—essentially a dean of students in charge of military training, counseling, mentorship, and the logistical care and feeding of the cadets—one of four such commanders that reported to the academy commandant. The assignment filled me with relief, happiness, and restored hope. But of course all that would come later.

My farewell from the White House was typical of what most military aides receive when they leave. My fellow military aides arranged an official farewell in the Oval Office with the president and a staff send-off of invited guests and friends in the Indian Treaty Room of the Old Executive Office Building.

I thought long and hard about whether to go along with the Oval Office ceremony. Very simply, I did not want to have to shake President Clinton's hand. I talked it over with my milaide brothers and decided to go to the ceremony if for no other reason than to give my wife, Nichole, and my parents the opportunity to come to the White House to mark the closing of my time there with the president.

My parents flew in from Atlanta, and as my wife, my parents, and I were ushered into the Oval Office, I caught a glance at President Clinton—and I couldn't believe it. He was eyeballing my wife as though she had just entered a singles bar. I was angered and immediately regretted being there and putting my wife in this situation.

The president presented me with the Defense Superior Service Medal for service to my country. He shook my hand and thanked me for my service to him and his administration. I thanked him for the opportunity to serve. To this day, I have not opened the box that I put my medal in immediately after receiving it.

As we exited the Oval Office, we ran into Mrs. Clinton. She was "on." She met my wife and parents, said her goodbyes to me, and then immediately chastised her personal aide for not putting my farewell on her schedule. It was vintage Hillary again, just as I knew her. My last two personal interactions with the Clintons completely encapsulated just who I knew them to be.

When the guard from the Uniformed Division of the Secret Service closed the gate behind me on my last day in the Clinton White House, all I could feel was tremendous relief. There was no sadness. There was only the sense that the man in the Oval Office had sown a whirlwind of destruction upon the integrity of our government, endangered our national security, and done enormous harm to the American military in which I served. He inherited a New World Order, where peace and opportunity were expected for the foreseeable future, but he left behind a world of disarray, where the symbol of America's wealth and modern prosperity—the World Trade Center towers in New York—would be destroyed within months of his departure. His administration's impact on the U.S. armed forces in terms of capability and readiness will truly be known only as this first decade of the new millennium concludes. He assumed command of the mightiest army the world has ever known, yet he left it eight years later as a significantly smaller force—significantly reduced in capability and decayed in infrastructure. His impact on the military in terms of morale and discipline may never be known. Members of the armed forces, when left with no other choice, tend to vote with their feet. During the Clinton administration, we voted with our feet in record numbers, myself included. Events since then have only strengthened these beliefs in me. And now, after those years of destruction, there is so much work to be done. I pray that it will.

APPENDICES

THE DANGERS WE STILL FACE

AS I STATED IN THE PREFACE, I am not speaking for the United States military establishment or its members. Again, I am but one of the countless thousands who served this country in the past two decades. From the outset, I did not intend to presume, or want the reader to presume, that this was anything other than one man's view as a career military officer privileged to participate in our nation's defense and serve directly for our commander in chief. My background as well as the anecdotes and the facts I've presented have led me to my own personal conclusions, opinions, and convictions.

My conclusions, however, have been developed and reinforced through countless informal and impromptu discussions with former military commanders, peers, and subordinates. The opinions I developed as a result of my interactions with the Clinton administration are the opinions of many. No military officer, no matter how politically motivated or apathetic, informed or naïve, comes into a situation of this magnitude without thinking of the consequences. The devastating effects the Clinton administration had on this nation's military left many of us talking.

It was only after I completed the manuscript for this project that I read Mr. Caspar Weinberger's 2001 book, In the Arena: A Memoir

of the 20th Century. *Weinberger was President Ronald Reagan's sec-*
retary of defense and is owed much credit for the remarkable triumph of
the Cold War. As I read page after page of Weinberger's memoirs, I was
gratified that the observations that had pained me during my White
House experiences were understood and shared by a professional states-
man and a man I had admired since early in my Air Force career.

In Chapter Seventeen of his book, Weinberger, more eloquently than
I ever could, sums up the true national security failings and fallout of the
Clinton presidency. And he does it from "outside the walls."

He rues the depth which Commander in Chief Clinton cut into the
military muscle of this country. He corroborates the weak and reckless
employment of U.S. military forces for largely domestic political gain.
And he describes the severely reduced U.S. capability that President
George W. Bush has inherited.

The larger picture he offers is that which I saw up close and personal.
The challenging future he paints is the one I also see. The conclusions he
draws are the ones I had already internalized as I walked out the East
Wing gate that last time. Through the experiences that I witnessed and
have documented, and from the lessons that Mr. Weinberger urges us to
relearn, may this nation recover and never again have our national secu-
rity interests treated with so much disdain and so little understanding.

With permission of the publisher, I offer this excerpt from Caspar
Weinberger's In the Arena *on "The Dangers We Still Face."*

Saddam Hussein has not yet tried to retake Kuwait, but his presence precludes any hope of lasting peace in the Mideast. Reli-
able intelligence tells us that Iraq continues to manufacture

chemical and biological weapons and to shop relentlessly for nuclear weapons, despite UN sanctions.

The Clinton administration, not surprisingly, was erratic and ineffective in dealing with the problem. Our "patience ran out" several times; we sought a "diplomatic solution" with a vicious killer who does not negotiate and who can never be believed or trusted; we occasionally dropped a few bombs or chased an Iraqi fighter jet out of the no-fly zone. But our credibility with our allies and against Saddam was seriously doubted because of Clinton's deep defense cuts, the irresoluteness of American policy, and the domestic political considerations that seemed to govern Clinton's foreign policy in the area.

We wondered why Saudi Arabia would not let us use its bases to support an attack that ultimately could have protected it and others in the region from Saddam Hussein's ever increasing capabilities to destroy them. I suspect the Saudis knew that, under Clinton, we would not do more than carry out a few days of token bombing, if that, if Iraq moved again into Kuwait or elsewhere.

All we sought was to reinsert UN inspectors into Iraq for a few days, with fewer restrictions placed on them, and yet Saddam continued to refuse even that. If we wanted to rid the world of the threats we faced in 1990 and 1991, we should have bombed every one of the disputed sites two or three times each, day and night, and we would have had to be prepared to ignore Saddam's inevitable lies about injured children.

Bombing alone would not oust this mass murderer, but if we were able to and did maintain a firm offensive, we could inflict enough damage to serve notice that we would not be bluffed any longer, thereby also warning other potential aggressors. We also could encourage and support opposition to Saddam inside and outside of Iraq. We should have eliminated or jailed Saddam himself—and still must do so, if we want any peace in the region.

Unfortunately, Iraq was not the only place where the Clinton administration abdicated its leadership responsibilities. Clinton's handling of the situation in Bosnia was a humiliation for the West comparable to the attempt to appease Hitler in the late 1930s.

How did this happen? When the uneasy alliance that was Yugoslavia broke apart, four nations—Croatia, Slovenia, Bosnia-Herzegovina, and Macedonia—claimed independence and were admitted to the UN. Serbia, meanwhile, embarked on its long-time goal of creating a Greater Serbia—controlling all of the former Yugoslavia of which it had also been a part. Serbia's allies in Bosnia cooperated with a shocking "ethnic cleansing" of Bosnia's Muslims, following Hitler's example.

The West's ultimate mistake was its failure to stop the Serbs at once. The problem again was the doctrine of limited objectives. Just as those who preached "containment" never intended to win the Cold War and those who sent our troops into Vietnam never planned to win, so too our approach to Serbia. We cautioned many times that we did not plan to defeat Serbia—only to stop its criminal atrocities.

President Clinton compounded this error when, shortly after his inauguration, he sent Warren Christopher to Europe, not to galvanize resistance to the aggression (as President Bush had done in the Gulf) but to inquire weakly what other countries would like to do. Naturally, none of them wanted to do very much, which sent a clear signal to the Serbs that they could pursue their aggression unhindered.

A routine UN arms embargo was put in place against Bosnia, but Russia continued to supply arms to the Serbs. For more than a year, UN and European "negotiators" bleated for cease-fires and "safe areas" and proposed various peace plans that awarded Serbia anywhere from 49 percent to 70 percent of Bosnia. The Serbs agreed to more than thirty cease-fire and safe-area proposals—and sometimes even kept their promises for as long as five or six hours.

The United States played an ignoble role, agreeing to giving the UN full command of the peacekeeping operation, which was manned by 23,000 lightly armed, ill-equipped troops scattered in hopelessly ineffective clusters and without effective rules of engagement. Predictably, these peacekeepers were attacked, ignored, overrun, and taken hostage, and the UN convoys of food and medicine were allowed to pass only when the Serbs gave permission.

This was the much-touted Dayton Agreement, signed in December 1995, which was supposed to create a stable, new "multiethnic Bosnian country." Instead, we accepted a partitioned Bosnia, which is what the Serbs wanted, with three parliaments (one federal, two regional), two separate armies, and two police forces, overseen by a rotating three-man presidency. Subsequent elections only emphasized that such a Rube Goldberg–like structure could not be built, let alone succeed.

Again, this demonstrated how easy it is to secure an agreement: just give up as much as the other party demands, and then we can have a big signing ceremony, proclaim ourselves peacemakers, and nominate our negotiators for the Nobel Peace Prize. Meanwhile, the victims of Serbia's aggression continue to suffer.

The United States has always been, and always should be, willing to accept the burdens of keeping peace and helping maintain freedom for ourselves and our allies. When, after two years of fatal, bumbling inaction, we cobbled together a paper agreement solving none of the conflicts that started the war, it was simply common sense to oppose deploying any soldiers, U.S. or NATO, to a mission inviting disaster—a "peacekeeping" mission where there was no peace to be kept.

Much earlier, we should have assembled a Gulf War–like coalition and told Serbia that its military targets would be mercilessly bombed by air forces under U.S. and NATO command if Serbia continued attacking civilian populations. When the brutality of Serb leader Slobodan Milosevic was again unleashed, this time in Kosovo, we ultimately did support NATO bombing, but with restrictions and restraints bound to make any operation ineffective.[*]

Ultimately, a new Serbian government ousted Milosevic from power. A few months later, he was turned over to the United Nations' War Crimes Tribunal, where he is now awaiting trial.

Another murderous regime sits in North Korea. It frightened the Clinton administration into another gross act of appeasement

---

[*] Targets could be bombed only after the approval of a large committee was secured.

(called a "framework agreement"), initiated by our own appeaser-negotiator, former president Jimmy Carter, who told the North Koreans he would try to get American sanctions against them lifted. The sanctions were lifted in the summer of 2000.

Time and time again, the Clinton administration inexplicably made concessions to North Korea in the hope the Communist regime would stop its nuclear weapons program. Under the "framework agreement," we even arranged to give the North Koreans two new nuclear reactors—ostensibly for more power, although the reactors are fully capable of producing plutonium, the very stuff of which nuclear weapons are made.

This absurd appeasement proceeded despite increasingly hostile actions by North Korea, including "test" launches over Japan of its new, long-range missiles—which can ultimately reach the United States—and thinly veiled threats against South Korea.

For example, in 1996, when the North sent a submarine with some twenty-five terrorists into South Korean waters, South Korea urged the United States to restart the valuable joint military exercises we had conducted with the South Korean armed forces from 1976 to 1994 (which we had stopped as part of the appeasement agreement we made with North Korea). But President Clinton merely urged "restraint" on both sides. Sadly, this is just one more example of the way in which the Clinton administration cavalierly disregarded and alienated our allies.

Aside from our increasingly strained relations with our allies, our own security was dangerously weakened by the inept Clinton as our commander in chief. Part of the problem was that

President Clinton did not understand the military, and worse, he did not like the military. Moreover, he did not recognize the importance of a strong defense.

Gone was our military strength that won the Cold War. By the late 1990s, we were spending less on new weapons and equipment than at any time in the last forty years. Spending on research and development programs had been cut by nearly 60 percent.

It has been said that we fought and won the Gulf War with Cap Weinberger's forces. In a 2000 interview with Rush Limbaugh, Dick Cheney summed up the current regrettable situation well: "We had 6 percent of our GNP going for defense during the Reagan years; [we have] less than 3 percent today. We used to have eighteen Army divisions; today we're down to ten. We used to have some twenty-four wings in the Air Force; we're down to thirteen today."

Each new administration appropriately begins with a re-examination of existing strategic policies. This process is under way with the new Bush administration, and the first result is usually a spate of rumors as to what has been decided, what new policies will be followed, and which existing policies will be changed.

There have already been many and varied reports, including that we are abandoning the "two-war" strategy and that we are offering to take out of service or destroy all of our largest and most accurate MX missiles, which were finally deployed after a major struggle with Congress and others in the 1980s.

Regardless of what our policy is called, we must have armed forces of the strength necessary to deter and conquer any threat.

If two attacks, leading to two wars that must necessarily be fought nearly simultaneously, are a possible threat, we must be strong enough to fight and win those two wars.

Such a threat is at least possible. China could decide it would no longer attempt to secure its "one China" goal by treaty or negotiation. Instead it could try to take Taiwan by force. Indeed, the continued increasing deployment along China's east coast of missiles facing and aimed at Taiwan cannot be ignored.

Should China attack Taiwan, North Korea, despite all of Clinton's attempts to offer what it wants, is equipped and positioned to launch another attack on South Korea.

The so-called two-war strategy was simply a convenient term for measuring and obtaining the kind and amount of deterrent military capability we might need. So long as giving up the two-war strategy does not mean giving up the military capabilities we may well need or the defense budgets big enough to support those capabilities, we need not worry too much.

But when we look at what has happened to the matchless military strength President Clinton inherited in January 1993, it is doubtful now that we could win one of those hypothetical two wars.

From 1985 to 2000, the total active-duty military personnel in our military went down by 34 percent.[*] Yet under Clinton, our forces were asked to serve in overseas assignments far more

---

[*] See Jack Spencer's "Building and Maintaining the Strength of America's Armed Forces," Chapter 10 of *Priorities for the President* by Baker Spring and Jack Spencer (Washington, DC: The Heritage Foundation, 2001).

often and for far longer than they should.* Few of these missions improved military training. Most were called "operations other than war," and our troops were "spending more and more time working on aging equipment at the expense of honing their important war-fighting skills."†

All of this was compounded by the Clinton "procurement holiday" and substantial cuts in the research and development work that earlier had produced the weapons with which we won the Gulf War.

Thus, today, our military faces extraordinary operation and maintenance costs for military hardware and weapons systems that it would be cheaper and more effective to replace with new models. New weapons systems not only have all the performance advantages of new technology, but they are increasingly built modularly, which means that they are far cheaper and easier to repair than older weapons systems. While our military's operations and maintenance costs are skyrocketing because of aging weapons systems and infrastructure, our vital military research and development budgets are suffering. The result is a

---

* Our forces "have been used over thirty times beyond normal training and operations since the end of the Cold War." This is compared with only ten such deployments in the preceding forty years. See Spring and Spencer, page 214. Dick Cheney also said, in his 2000 Rush Limbaugh interview: "We've given the forces a lot of assignments they didn't used to have, the so-called peacekeeping assignments. What that means is that the guys are away from home all the time. The thing you hear about is 'the birthday problem.' A guy will tell you, 'Look, I missed my kid's last three birthdays because I was away from home. So I'm leaving. I can't take it anymore.'"

† General H. H. Shelton, Chairman of the Joint Chiefs of Staff, testimony to U.S. Senate Armed Services Committee, September 27, 2000.

military whose operational capability is in serious danger of exponential decline. The Clinton administration inexcusably hollowed out our military capability and has left President Bush with the tab for making good Clinton's deficits on what should have been spent.

Not surprisingly, all of this has contributed to a loss in morale and a most worrisome difficulty in recruitment and retention of troops—something we never experienced during the Reagan buildup in the 1980s.*

We need to return to major increases in defense spending overall, and in particular, we need to rebuild the Reagan-era Navy. Our Navy today is roughly half as large as it was in the Reagan years, and yet the most immediate challenges we will likely face are naval challenges, since our most likely areas of conflict are separated from us by vast oceans. We have to be able to move our armed forces around the map, so we need a drastic upgrading of our air- and sea-lift capabilities. It takes six or seven years to build and fully deploy—with trained crews—aircraft carriers and nuclear submarines. We need to be building them now. It takes two or three years to build and deploy combat aircraft. We need to be building them now as well. After the years of Clinton neglect, we are seeing a disastrous de facto build-down—by failing to replace out-of-date ships and aircraft—of major and highly disturbing proportions.

With the election of George W. Bush, things are improving, and I expect that his commitment to our military will alleviate

---

* See Spring and Spencer, pages 217–218.

many of these problems. Still, it will take time and continued advocacy and determination to repair the damage wrought by eight years of the Clinton administration.

President Bush has also taken to heart the highest defense priority we should have—building a defense against intercontinental ballistic nuclear missiles and missiles with chemical or biological warheads.* Russia alone has an estimated 15,000 to 20,000 nuclear warheads.†

The Reagan administration worked for years to build a genuine, nationwide defense against these incoming intercontinental and intermediate-range missiles, but we were continually hampered by demands from Democrats and some Republicans that everything be "ABM Treaty–compliant" (read "totally ineffective"). No one in the Reagan administration was suggesting that we violate our treaty obligations. What was repeatedly urged was that we use the specific provisions of the treaty itself to get us out of it, as legally permitted, so that we can build and deploy effective defenses.

President Clinton and his State Department remained wedded to the flawed 1972 ABM Treaty, despite intelligence reports—and later, Russia's own admission—that the Soviet Union had violated the treaty almost from the beginning by deploying its giant radar at Krasnoyarsk. In September 1997,

---

* For the best description of the nature and size of the ballistic missile threat we face, see *The Ballistic Missile Threat Handbook* by Jack Spencer (Washington, DC: The Heritage Foundation, 2000).

† *Military Almanac* (Washington, DC: Center for Defense Information, 1999), 9.

Secretary of State Madeleine Albright signed agreements designating Russia, Kazakhstan, Belarus, and Ukraine as our ABM Treaty partners in place of the collapsed USSR. Strobe Talbott, her Russophile deputy secretary, said as late as May 2000 that we meant to adhere to and strengthen the ABM Treaty. None of these new agreements, however, was ever submitted to the Senate. And now, with President Bush, thankfully they will not be; already in his young administration, it is clear that capable, tough-minded professionals such as National Security Advisor Condoleezza Rice, Secretary of State Colin Powell, and Secretary of Defense Donald Rumsfeld have returned to putting the legitimate interests of the United States and our allies first. I have high hopes for the new administration and see it as a worthy inheritor—after the lamentable Clinton years—of the work I tried to achieve as secretary of defense for Ronald Reagan. This administration knows that peace comes through strength, that America must lead, and that nothing is more important than our national defense.

Two steps are necessary to gain any real security: we must reject any ABM succession agreements and announce that we will no longer be bound by the old ABM Treaty, and we must move ahead with the research and subsequent deployment that will give us and our allies a viable defense against nuclear, chemical, and biological weapons. The Clinton administration and its faint-hearted supporters stood in the way....

President Clinton, inclined as he was to conduct policy by poll, should have noted that polls showed that a horrified majority of Americans were unaware that we currently have no effective defense against nuclear missile attack. Moreover, nearly 70 percent of respondents considered having a strong military to be very important and said that they were willing to pay the taxes necessary to ensure that the United States remains a global superpower.

The American people understand, if President Clinton did not, that the fact that we won the Cold War has changed—not removed—the various threats we could face.

PRESIDENT CLINTON FOREIGN POLICY CHRONOLOGY, 1993–2001

1993

February 26: In New York, the World Trade Center is bombed by Islamic terrorists. A car bomb planted in an underground garage kills six people and leaves one thousand injured. Investigators believe the mastermind of the attack, Ramzi Yousef, is financially connected to Osama bin Laden.

April 12: NATO (North Atlantic Treaty Organization) air forces begin enforcing the UN-mandated no-fly zone over Bosnia, involving sixty U.S., French, and Dutch warplanes.

April 9–18: In Iraq, U.S. planes bomb Iraqi antiaircraft sites that had tracked and attacked U.S. aircraft.

April 13: U.S. forces in association with NATO enforce the ban on all unauthorized military flights over Bosnia-Herzegovina.

May 4: In Somalia, Operation Restore Hope is replaced by the United Nations Security Council operation UNOSOM II (United Nations Operation in Somalia), with enforcement powers and a mandate to disarm warring factions, in accordance with the Addis Ababa agreements of January

1993. Out of 22,700 multinational troops and logistics personnel, up to 2,900 are U.S. forces, primarily combat support personnel assigned to the UN Logistics Support Command. Restore Hope was established under United States command in December 1992 to establish a secure environment for humanitarian relief operations. Some 25,800 U.S. military forces were included among the 37,000 peacekeepers.

June 19: U.S. aircraft fire on an Iraqi antiaircraft site displaying hostile intent.

June 26: The United States attacks the Iraqi Intelligence Service Headquarters in Baghdad, launching twenty-three Tomahawk Cruise Missiles in retaliation for an attempted assassination of the former U.S. president George Bush while he visited Kuwait two months earlier. The assassination plot was hatched by Iraqi agents.

July 9: UN protection forces, including 350 U.S. soldiers, are deployed to participate in the UN protection for the former Yugoslav Republic of Macedonia.

August 3: An Army Ranger task force of more than 1,100 soldiers is deployed to Somalia as a "quick reaction force."

August 31: The Oslo Accords are agreed to by Israel and the Palestine Liberation Organization during secret talks in Norway. After forty-five years of conflict, the two agree to recognize each other. Within days, Yasser Arafat signs a letter recognizing Israel and renouncing violence.

September 13: The Oslo Accords are signed by Israeli and Palestinian leaders at a White House ceremony.

October 3: In Somalia, eighteen American soldiers are killed in a Mogadishu firefight with irregular forces loyal to warlord Mohammed Aidid. Some 500 to 1,000 of Aidid's fighters are killed by U.S. troops.

October 7: President Clinton announces that the United States will withdraw all combat forces and most logistics units from Somalia by March 31, 1994.

1994

January 6: President Clinton labels three types of satellites as "civilian," thus circumventing sanctions on China in order to allow exports to proceed.

January 12: Under media pressure, President Clinton asks that a special prosecutor be named to investigate the Whitewater scandal. A week later, Attorney General Janet Reno names Robert Fiske as special prosecutor.

February 28: U.S. military aircraft under NATO shoot down four Serbian Galeb planes in the former Yugoslavia while patrolling the no-fly zone.

April 10–11: NATO-led U.S. warplanes strike Bosnian Serb forces in Gorazde.

April 12: U.S. combat-equipped forces are deployed to Burundi to assist with the evacuation of U.S. embassy personnel and other citizens from Rwanda.

May 4: In Cairo, Israeli prime minister Yitzhak Rabin and Yasser Arafat sign the Agreement on the Gaza Strip and Jericho Area, formally setting terms for the withdrawal of Israeli military forces.

May 6: Paula Jones files a sexual harassment lawsuit against President Clinton.

June 3: President Clinton issues Executive Order 12919, on "National Defense Industrial Resources Preparedness," which consolidates previous executive orders to give the executive branch sweeping powers for emergency control of food resources, farm equipment and commercial fertilizer, health resources, all forms of civil transportation, water resources, construction material, and labor supply. The order gives the director of FEMA (Federal Emergency Management Agency) a key role in developing and implementing the policy. Critics claim this order is extraconstitutional in scope and could grant a president virtually dictatorial powers.

July 13: President Clinton issues presidential waivers under P.L. 101-246 to allow U.S. satellites to be launched from Chinese rockets.

July 22: In Rwanda, U.S. forces begin a three-month intervention to assist nongovernmental and international organizations to provide relief to refugees of the civil war and to assist with the deployment of UN peacekeeping troops. By mid-August, U.S. troops participating at the peak of the mission total 3,600, with most deployed outside of Rwanda.

August 5: U.S. aircraft, operating under NATO and acting upon requests of UN protective forces, attack Bosnian Serb heavy weapons in Sarajevo's heavy-weapons exclusion zone.

September 19: Some 20,000 U.S. forces enter Haiti under code name Operation Uphold Democracy, as the lead force in the multinational operation to restore Jean-Bertrand Aristide to power.

October 15: President Clinton lifts sanctions he had imposed on China for selling missile technology to Pakistan.

November 1: A newly operational Afghan militant force, called the Taliban, created by Pakistan's Inter-Service Intelligence Agency around Islamic schools, or madrasas, and funded with Saudi Arabian resources, emerges from northwest Pakistan and captures Kandahar, the Pashtun tribal center in southeastern Afghanistan.

November 1: President Clinton issues a waiver on sanctions on China for missile-technology exports.

November 10: Iraq accepts the UN-designated land border with Kuwait as well as Kuwaiti sovereignty as confirmed by UN Security Council Resolution 833.

November 19: The UN Security Council approves Resolution 958, which authorizes the use of air power to support the UN Protection Force in Croatia.

December 12: China reportedly begins to transfer ring magnets to an unsafely guarded nuclear facility in Pakistan. This violates the Nuclear Nonproliferation Treaty and contravenes U.S. laws that require sanctions.

December 22: President Clinton announces that the U.S. Army peacekeeping force in Macedonia will be replaced by five hundred soldiers from the 1st Cavalry Division.

1995

January 9: Bernard Schwartz, chairman of Loral Space and
Communications Corporation, signs a letter to the president
advocating the shift of satellite export responsibility from
the Department of State to the Department of Commerce.

February 27: In Somalia, some 1,800 U.S. combat forces
arrive in Mogadishu to assist with the removal of the
United Nations Operations in Somalia (UNOSOM II)
peacekeeping operation.

March 3: The UNOSOM II international peacekeeping force
is withdrawn from Somalia, in the midst of continuing
instability.

March 8: Three unidentified gunmen kill two U.S. diplomats
and wound a third in Karachi, Pakistan.

March 31: The U.S.-led peace operation in Haiti gives way to
a United Nations peacekeeping operation, called the UN
Mission in Haiti, or UNMH.

April 19: In Oklahoma City, a terrorist attack on the federal
building by American extremists kills 168 and wounds
hundreds more.

May 3: President Clinton issues Presidential Decision Directive 25 (PDD-25), in secretive classified form. The directive
outlines U.S. roles in UN-authorized and other international "peacekeeping" activities. The document, which
effects the deployment of U.S. military forces into hostile
zones, is denied to the public and to the U.S. Congress,
which has constitutional responsibility to approve military
deployments. The directive calls for the elimination of the

War Powers Act provision requiring withdrawal of U.S. troops within sixty days, without congressional approval. That provision is not addressed by Congress.

June 3: NATO and other European Union countries agree to plans for a rapid-reaction force of up to 10,000 troops to protect UN peacekeepers in Bosnia. The United States offers to provide air support, intelligence, transport, and other equipment, and rules out ground troops.

June 8: A U.S. Marine search-and-rescue team successfully rescues Captain Scott O'Grady of the U.S. Air Force, shot down by a Bosnian Serb missile and stranded in Bosnia for six days.

June 25: In Haiti, first-round parliamentary and municipal elections are held. Although deadly violence does not occur, election observers state that there are numerous irregularities, including ballot burning in some locations.

August 8: Two of Saddam Hussein's sons-in-law, both key aides, defect and are granted political asylum abroad. One of the defectors, Hussein Kamel, is the principal architect of Iraq's programs of mass-destruction weapons and claims that Saddam intends to invade Kuwait and Saudi Arabia.

August 30: NATO begins a campaign of massive air strikes against Bosnian Serb military targets around Sarajevo under Operation Deliberate Force, which lasts for around one month.

September 28: The Israeli-Palestinian Interim Agreement on the West Bank is signed in Washington. Following the signing, President Clinton hosts a summit attended by Jordan's

King Hussein, Egypt's President Hosni Mubarak, Israel's Prime Minister Yitzhak Rabin, and PLO chairman Yasser Arafat.

October 9: After long debate within the administration, in which the Defense Department, CIA, and State Department oppose American satellites' being launched on Chinese rockets, President Clinton initials a classified order maintaining the State Department's authority over the Commerce Department on such launchings.

November 1: In Dayton, Ohio, "proximity peace talks" begin between the United States and other contact group countries to resolve the Balkan conflict.

November 4: Israeli prime minister Yitzhak Rabin is assassinated in Tel Aviv by an Israeli university student.

November 13: A bomb hidden in a van explodes at the U.S. military headquarters in Riyadh, Saudi Arabia, killing seven, including five Americans.

November 21: The Dayton Peace Accords are signed to end the Balkan conflict.

December 17: Presidential elections are held in Haiti. Although former president Aristide is not permitted to run, his protégé, René Préval, wins with 89 percent of the votes cast. The vote is marred by only a 28 percent voter turnout and by the boycott of the election by many parties.

1996

February 6: President Clinton issues a waiver to lift sanctions and permit four satellites, including a Loral product, to be launched on Chinese rockets despite the January reports that China continues to export nuclear technology to Pakistan. On the same day, Clinton's friend—and Chinese Triad mafia member—Charlie Trie attends a White House coffee with Wang Jun, China's top military-industrial arms dealer, who had a multibillion-dollar stake in getting access to American satellites.

February 14: On liftoff, the Chinese launch of its Long March rocket fails, killing several people and destroying a $126 million U.S. satellite belonging to Loral Space and Communications Corp.

March 10–11: The United States deploys two carrier battle groups to the waters off Taiwan, calling China's live-fire exercises, intended to intimidate Taiwan, "reckless" and "risky."

March 14: The Clinton administration announces a decision to move a commercial communications satellite from the Munitions List to the Commerce Control List of dual-use items. The export license is moved from the Department of State to the Department of Commerce.

April 5: The *Los Angeles Times* reports that the Clinton administration tacitly approved a shipment of Iranian arms to the Bosnian government in 1994.

April 9: President Clinton orders U.S. military forces to Liberia to evacuate "private U.S. citizens and certain third-country nationals who had taken refuge in the U.S. Embassy compound" because of the "deterioration of the security situation and the resulting threat to American citizens."

May 10: Loral completes an engineering report that instructs China how to improve its faulty rockets and missiles, including solving fatal problems in guidance systems. This assistance enhances the ability of Chinese ICBMs to hit American cities with precision.

May 10: Loral's commission studying the failure of China's Long March missile launch completes a preliminary review that is shared with China, finding that the cause of the accident was an electrical flaw in the electronic flight-control system. The report allegedly discusses weaknesses in the Chinese rocket's guidance-and-control systems.

May 10: Sudan expels Osama bin Laden because of international pressure applied by the United States and Saudi Arabia. He returns to Afghanistan.

May 20: President Clinton reports to Congress the continual deployment of U.S. military forces to evacuate the U.S. embassy in Liberia and to respond to the various isolated "attacks on the American Embassy complex."

May 23: President Clinton reports to Congress the deployment of U.S. military personnel to evacuate "private citizens and certain U.S. government employees," and to provide "enhanced security for the American Embassy in Bangui" in the Central African Republic.

May 23: The Clinton administration announces that China will not be sanctioned for transferring the ring magnets to Pakistan, saying that there is no evidence that the Chinese government (as opposed to a state-owned company) has "willfully aided or abetted" Pakistan's nuclear weapons program.

June 1: In Hong Kong, Clinton donor Johnny Chung meets China Aerospace Corp. executive Liu Chaoying, a lieutenant colonel in the People's Liberation Army who attended counterintelligence school. Her company builds satellites and rockets and provides equipment for China's nuclear tests. The company also owns China Great Wall Industry Corp., which had been sanctioned by the United States in 1991 and 1993 for selling missiles to Pakistan.

June 23: President Clinton waives sanctions under P.L. 101-246 for the Asia-Pacific Mobile Telecommunications (APMT) satellite to be exported for launch from China.

June 25: Khobar Towers, a military housing facility in Dhahran, Saudi Arabia, is attacked as a fuel truck carrying a bomb explodes, killing nineteen U.S. military personnel and wounding 515 more. Several groups claim responsibility for the attack.

July 9: President Clinton waives sanctions under P.L. 101-246, allowing the Globalstar satellite to be exported for launch from China.

July 19–26: Liu Chaoying, a Chinese aerospace executive, arrives in the United States and at the home of Democratic fundraiser Eli Broad, and subsequently shakes President Clinton's hand for a picture taken with him. Liu and Johnny Chung incorporate Marswell Investment, Inc., similar to a Hong Kong company that is a front for the political department of the Chinese People's Liberation Army (PLA). Deposits to Marswell accounts reportedly travel from the PLA to U.S. Democratic Party causes.

August 23: Osama bin Laden issues a Declaration of Jihad, or religious war, against the United States, and calls for support of Islamic revolutionary groups around the world.

September 3–4: U.S. forces launch forty-four cruise missiles at military targets in southern Iraq. President Clinton announces the widening of the no-fly zones.

September 27: The Taliban movement captures Kabul, Afghanistan's capital, and gains control of 90 percent of the country. The mostly Pashtun tribal Taliban are resisted in northern Afghanistan primarily by Tajik, Uzbek, and Hazara ethnic groups. The Clinton administration hopes the Taliban will bring stability to Afghanistan.

December 20: The NATO-led Implementation Force (IFOR) peacekeeping mission ends in Bosnia, and the UN-mandated Stabilization Force (SFOR) mission begins. The 54,000 troops of IFOR—which include 16,200 U.S. troops in Bosnia and some 6,000 support personnel stationed in the region—are replaced by just 18,000 SFOR troops. The U.S. contingent is reduced to 3,600 troops in Bosnia and an additional 1,000 personnel stationed in neighboring countries to participate in NATO operations in the Balkans.

1997

February 23: As punishment against the "enemies" of Palestine, a Palestinian gunman opens fire on the observation deck of the Empire State Building in New York City. One person is killed and six others are wounded before he turns the gun on himself.

March 13: President Clinton utilizes U.S. military forces to evacuate certain U.S. government employees and private American citizens from Tirana, Albania, and to enhance security for the U.S. embassy in that city.

March 25: U.S. military forces deploy to Congo and Gabon for a standby evacuation of Americans from Zaire.

May 15: President Clinton issues the secret Presidential Decision Directive 56 (PDD-56), "The Clinton Administration Policy on Managing Complex Contingency Operations," which purportedly guides the policy for PDD-25 on the U.S. role in international peacekeeping operations. A controversial feature of the directive is that UN-associated nongovernmental organizations (NGOs) are given a "voice in the field" through the creation of a "Civilian-Military Operation Center." The directive also urges the inclusion of the NGOs "in the planning and policymaking circles in Washington."

May 16: A classified report at the Department of Defense's Defense Technology Security Administration (DTSA) concludes that Loral and Hughes Electronics Corp. have transferred expertise to China that significantly enhances the reliability of its nuclear ballistic missiles and that "United States national security has been harmed" (cited in the April 13, 1998, *New York Times*).

May 29–30: President Clinton orders U.S. military forces deployed to Freetown, Sierra Leone, to prepare for and undertake the evacuation of certain U.S. government employees and private U.S. citizens.

July 5–7: In Cambodia, the former Khmer Rouge co–prime minister stages a coup against the freely elected royalist prime minister, Prince Ranariddh.

September 9: The Department of Justice begins a criminal investigation into allegations that Loral and Hughes illegally passed technical assistance to China.

September 10–12: With the Middle East peace process stalled for more than one year, Secretary of State Madeleine Albright makes her first official trip to the Middle East.

September 26: Representing the administration, Secretary of State Madeleine Albright signs three agreements related to the Anti–Ballistic Missile (ABM) Treaty at the United Nations. Defense experts criticize the agreements as threatening U.S. national security by reimposing restrictions found in the defunct 1972 ABM Treaty between the United States and the Soviet Union, including restrictions on a national missile defense system. Although the treaty expired in 1991, with the fall of the Soviet Union, the Clinton administration continues to observe the requirements of the treaty as policy.

November: President Clinton issues the highly classified Presidential Decision Directive 60 (PDD-60), which involves a significant change in U.S. strategic nuclear doctrine by formally abandoning guidelines issued by the Reagan administration in 1981 that the United States must be prepared to fight and win a protracted nuclear war.

December 5: President Clinton issues a "presidential determination" waiving provisions of the Anti-Terrorism Act of
1987 to authorize the reopening of the Palestine Liberation
Organization's office in Washington, D.C.

December 19: Monica Lewinsky is issued a subpoena to
appear at a deposition in the Paula Jones suit.

1998

January 26: President Clinton declares publicly, regarding
Lewinsky, "I did not have sexual relations with that
woman."

February 23: Bin Laden issues a joint declaration with the
Egyptian Islamic group Al Jihad, the Jihad Movement in
Bangladesh, and the Jamiat-ul-Ulema-e-Pakistan under the
banner of the "World Islamic Front," which states that Muslims should kill Americans, including civilians—anywhere
in the world.

April 16–17: The U.S. ambassador to the United Nations, Bill
Richardson, visits Afghanistan and Pakistan. In Afghanistan,
he asks the Northern Alliance resistance to stop its successful offensive against the Taliban and their al-Qaeda allies.
He is rebuffed by the Taliban when he asks them to hand
over Osama bin Laden. Richardson calls for an end of military supplies to all warring factions, and voices support for a
religious clergy conference, or *ulama,* called for by Pakistan
to discuss peace. The arms embargo is largely honored by
the Northern Alliance resistance. Pakistan, however, steps

up arms supplies to the Taliban and sends in military reinforcements from the army and religious schools. Within a
few months, the Taliban and al-Qaeda regain a military
advantage and, with support from Pakistani air power,
capture most of the Northern Alliance areas of resistance.

June 8: A U.S. grand jury investigation of bin Laden, initiated
in 1996, issues a sealed indictment, charging bin Laden
with "conspiracy to attack defense utilities of the United
States." Prosecutors charge that bin Laden heads a terrorist
organization called al-Qaeda, "the base," and is a major
financier of Islamic terrorists around the world.

August 6: Monica Lewinsky testifies under immunity to a
grand jury.

August 7: U.S. embassies in Nairobi, Kenya, and Dar es
Salaam, Tanzania, are bombed simultaneously, killing 224,
including 12 Americans, and injuring more than 5,000. It is
determined that Osama bin Laden is responsible for the
attacks.

August 17: President Clinton undergoes four hours of questioning before a grand jury. Afterward, he says in a televised
speech, "I did have a relationship with Ms. Lewinsky that
was not appropriate."

August 20: President Clinton orders synchronized air strikes
in Afghanistan and Sudan. In Sudan, the United States
strikes a pharmaceutical plant suspected of being a chemical weapons factory. In Afghanistan, cruise missiles strike
camps used by the Osama bin Laden terrorist organization
after convincing information is found linking the bin Laden

organization to the bombings of the U.S. embassies in
Kenya and Tanzania on August 7, 1998.

September 9: Kenneth Starr tells House leaders that he has
found "substantial and credible information...that may
constitute grounds for an impeachment."

September 15: Following the Taliban and al-Qaeda capture of
Bamiyan, the Hazara tribal stronghold in central Afghanistan, massive atrocities are committed against the civilian
population. On Afghanistan's western border, Iran masses
200,000 troops in response to the Taliban's northern offensive, which is backed by Pakistan.

September 21: The *New York Times* reports that, in August, a
small group of presidential advisors met with Clinton,
reportedly with evidence that bin Laden wished to obtain
weapons of mass destruction and chemical weapons to use
against U.S. installations.

September 23: The UN Security Council adopts Resolution
1199, demanding a cessation of hostilities in Kosovo and
warning that "additional measures" to restore peace will be
considered.

October 15–23: At the Wye River Conference in Maryland,
President Clinton and Secretary Albright broker an inten-
sive conference-ending all-night session between Israeli
and Palestinian leaders. The meeting results in the Wye
River Memorandum, which is signed at the White House
on October 23.

November 13: President Clinton agrees to pay Paula Jones
$850,000 to drop her sexual harassment lawsuit.

November 30: President Clinton hosts a Middle East Donors Conference in Washington, at which some forty nations pledge over $3 billion to the Palestinian Authority.

December 11–12: The House Judiciary Committee approves four articles of impeachment against President Clinton, which involve perjury and obstruction of justice in the Jones case.

December 19: President Clinton is impeached; the House of Representatives approves two articles of impeachment.

December 20: Polls show that President Clinton's approval ratings continue to rise.

1999

January 13: The *Washington Times* reports that President Clinton backed away from an announcement on funding the first part of a deployed national missile defense after U.S. attacks on Iraq prompted Russia to halt its ratification of the START II arms treaty.

February 12: The U.S. Senate votes to acquit President Clinton on both impeachment charges.

March 24: U.S. military forces in coalition with NATO allies commence a seventy-eight-day bombing campaign against Serbia and Serb forces in Kosovo in response to the Yugoslav government's campaign of violence and repression against the ethnic Albanian population in Kosovo.

May 7: NATO airplanes mistakenly bomb the Chinese embassy in Belgrade, killing seven. China accuses the United States of conducting a deliberate attack.

May 25: The U.S. House of Representatives Select Committee on U.S. National Security and Military/Commercial Concerns with the People's Republic of China (the Cox Commission) releases a three-volume report detailing the transfer of sensitive "dual-use" U.S. military-related technologies to China. The report includes the satellite/rocket-related cases pertaining to the Loral and Hughes companies. "The seriousness of these findings and their enormous significance to our national security," the commission states, includes theft of some of America's most sensitive technologies, including nuclear weapons design.

May 27: The Russian Duma adopts a resolution condemning the NATO actions and postpones ratification of the START II treaty.

June 10: NATO suspends bombing in Kosovo after Serb forces begin to withdraw.

June 11–12: Kosovo Forces (KFOR) troops begin entering Kosovo. Russian troops arrive in Pristina three hours before NATO troops arrive in Kosovo.

June 20: Serb forces completely withdraw from Kosovo, which signals NATO to end its bombing campaign in the former Republic of Yugoslavia.

July 14–20: Israeli prime minister Ehud Barak visits the United States for the first time since taking office on July 6. He and President Clinton pledge to make peace a top priority.

July 15: A congressionally mandated Commission to Assess the Ballistic Missile Threat to the United States, led by former secretary of defense Donald Rumsfeld, concludes that

"Ballistic missiles armed with WMD [weapons of mass destruction] payloads pose [an immediate] strategic threat to the United States." The commission's findings are in stark contrast to the Clinton administration's definitive 1995 National Intelligence Estimate that there would be "no threat from long-range ballistic missiles for at least 15 years." The report adds, "The threat to the U.S. posed by these emerging capabilities is broader, more mature and evolving more rapidly than has been reported in estimates and reports by the [Clinton administration] Intelligence community."

July 19: President Clinton reports to Congress that, "consistent with the War Powers Resolution," about 6,200 U.S. military personnel continue to participate in the NATO-led SFOR operation in Bosnia, and another 2,200 troops will support SFOR from other parts of the region. In addition, U.S. military personnel will remain in Macedonia in support of the international security presence in Kosovo.

November 2: At a ceremony in Oslo commemorating the anniversary of Yitzhak Rabin's assassination, President Clinton meets with Barak and Arafat, who agree to designate February 13, 2000, as the target for achieving a framework agreement on the permanent status of peace issues.

December 15: President Clinton reports to Congress that, "consistent with the War Powers Resolution," 8,000 U.S. combat-equipped military personnel will continue to serve as part of the NATO-led KFOR security force in Kosovo. Another 1,500 U.S. troops are deployed in other parts of the region in support roles.

2000

February 25: President Clinton announces that a small number of U.S. military personnel will be assigned as part of the United Nations Transitional Administration in East Timor. The contingent includes three military observers and one judge advocate. The president also assigns a thirty-troop military support group to facilitate and coordinate U.S. military activities on the island.

October 12: In Aden, Yemen, an explosive-laden boat blows up alongside the USS *Cole,* killing seventeen American sailors. Al-Qaeda operatives and bin Laden are suspected.

November 26: In Haiti, Jean-Bertrand Aristide is elected president again, although the election is boycotted by most of the opposition.

December 18: President Clinton reports to Congress that, "consistent with the War Powers Resolution," 5,600 U.S. troops remain as part of the NATO-led KFOR security force in Kosovo. Another 500 U.S. support troops are deployed in neighboring Macedonia.

2001

September 11: Terrorists, coordinated by Osama bin Laden's al-Qaeda network, attack New York's World Trade Center and the Pentagon by flying hijacked American commercial passenger airplanes into the buildings.

REPORTS AND SCORES

FIELD GRADE OFFICER PERFORMANCE REPORT

I. RATEE IDENTIFICATION DATA *(Read AFI 36-2402 carefully before filling in any item)*

1. NAME *(Last, First, Middle Initial)* Patterson, Robert B.	2. SSN	3. GRADE LT COL	4. DAFSC 16R4

5. PERIOD OF REPORT From: 11 May 96 Thru: 10 May 97	6. NO. DAYS SUPERVISION 359	7. REASON FOR REPORT Annual

8. ORGANIZATION, COMMAND, LOCATION White House Military Office, The White House, Washington, D.C. 20500 (ELM)	9. PAS CODE HH3VFRN1

II. UNIT MISSION DESCRIPTION

Provides direct support to the President of the United States.

III. JOB DESCRIPTION

1. DUTY TITLE:
Air Force Aide to the President

2. KEY DUTIES, TASKS, AND RESPONSIBILITIES:
Emergency Actions Officer: Develops and executes plans for contingencies ranging from medical emergencies to national security crises; safeguards and is responsible for the President's Emergency Satchel--"the Football." White House Military Office Operations Officer: Coordinates the employment of all military assets used in support of the President. Aide-de-Camp: Military escort for the President at official functions, formal ceremonies, and during travel; acts as personal assistant to the President during evenings, weekends, and visits to Camp David; other duties and functions as required by the President.

IV. IMPACT ON MISSION ACCOMPLISHMENT

- America's finest, a standout leader--one of only five elite Presidential Military Aides
  -- Trusted advisor and agent; responsible for the President's Emergency Satchel--"the Football"
  -- Expert on all phases of contingency plans for protection and continuity of the Presidency
- Masterful planner! Coordinated all military assets and potential contingency operations for 31 Presidential visits to 35 cities across the nation and abroad--diplomatic, thorough, and discerning
  -- Adroitly managed all military involvement for 1996 Asian Pacific Economic Conference in Manila, RP
- Ambassador in blue--articulate, poised, and confident when interacting with Cabinet officials, high level staff, Presidential guests, the Joint Chiefs, and foreign heads of state
- Trusted Aide-de-Camp for First Family retreats to Camp David, Arkansas, and St. Thomas, Virgin Is.

V. PERFORMANCE FACTORS	DOES NOT MEET STANDARDS	MEETS STANDARDS
1. Job Knowledge Has knowledge required to perform duties effectively. Strives to improve knowledge. Applies knowledge to handle nonroutine situations.	☐	☒
2. Leadership Skills Sets and enforces standards. Motivates subordinates. Works well with others. Fosters teamwork. Displays initiative. Self-confident. Has respect and confidence of subordinates. Fair and consistent in evaluation of subordinates.	☐	☒
3. Professional Qualities Exhibits loyalty, discipline, dedication, integrity, honesty, and officership. Adheres to Air Force standards. Accepts personal responsibility. Is fair and objective.	☐	☒
4. Organizational Skills Plans, coordinates, schedules, and uses resources effectively. Schedules work for self and others equitably and effectively. Anticipates and solves problems. Meets suspenses.	☐	☒
5. Judgement and Decisions Makes timely and accurate decisions. Emphasizes logic in decision making. Retains composure in stressful situations. Recognizes opportunities and acts to take advantage of them.	☐	☒
6. Communication Skills Listens, speaks, and writes effectively.	☐	☒

AF FORM 707A, OCT 95 *(EF -V1)* *(PerFORM PRO)*   PREVIOUS EDITION IS OBSOLETE.

My first of two field grade officer performance reports, with assessments of my performance from President Clinton.

VI. RATER OVERALL ASSESSMENT

Lieutenant Colonel Buzz Patterson has earned my personal and professional respect and surpasses the high expectations placed on a Presidential Military Aide. I have the utmost faith in his abilities and implicitly trust him to execute the emergency actions necessary to ensure the continuity of the Presidency and the ntinued authority of the Commander-in-Chief. A consummate team player, he has impressed us with his ability to react quickly to changing situations and to do so with extraordinary discretion and tact. When I suffered my knee injury in Florida, Buzz quickly and responsibly coordinated my movement to the hospital while notifying senior staff. At my side, he has coordinated several foreign leaders and acts as my personal aide when I get away to Camp David or vacation. Buzz is a future leader the Air Force can be proud of. After he commands a flying squadron, send him to National War College—he's earned it!

Last performance feedback was accomplished on: **28 Nov 96**   (consistent with the direction in AFI 36-2402.)
(If not accomplished, state the reason)

NAME, GRADE, BR OF SVC, ORGN, COMD & LOCATION WILLIAM J. CLINTON The White House Washington, D.C. 20500	DUTY TITLE President of the United States		DATE 5/16/97
	SSN	SIGNATURE *William J Clinton*	

VII. ADDITIONAL RATER OVERALL ASSESSMENT   ☒ CONCUR   NONCONCUR

He is very impressive and professional — I have a high regard for him and his potential.

NAME, GRADE, BR OF SVC, ORGN, COMD & LOCATION	DUTY TITLE		DATE
	SSN	SIGNATURE	

I. REVIEWER   CONCUR   NONCONCUR

Rater is also reviewer.

NAME, GRADE, BR OF SVC, ORGN, COMD & LOCATION	DUTY TITLE		DATE
	SSN	SIGNATURE	

Instructions

All: Recommendations must be based on performance and the potential based on that performance. Promotion recommendations are prohibited. Do not comment on completion of or enrollment in PME, advanced education, previous or anticipated promotion recommendations on AF Form 709, OER indorsement levels, family activities, marital status, race, sex, ethnic origin, age, or religion.

Rater: Focus your evaluation in Section IV on what the officer did, how well he or she did it and how the officer contributed to mission accomplishment. Write in concise "bullet" format. Your comments in Section VI may include recommendations for augmentation or assignment.

Additional Rater: Carefully review the rater's evaluation to ensure it is accurate, unbiased and uninflated. If you disagree, you may ask the rater to review his or her evaluation. You may not direct a change in the evaluation. If you still disagree with the rater, mark "NON-CONCUR" and explain. You may include recommendations for augmentation or assignment.

Reviewer: Carefully review the rater's and additional rater's ratings and comments. If their evaluations are accurate, unbiased and uninflated, mark the form "CONCUR" and sign the form. If you disagree with previous evaluators, you may ask them to review their evaluations. You may not direct them to change their appraisals. If you still disagree with the additional rater, mark "NONCONCUR" and explain in Section VIII. Do not use "NONCONCUR" simply to provide comments on the report.

IX. ACQUISITION EXAMINER/AIR FORCE ADVISOR (Indicate applicable review by marking the appropriate box(es).)		ACQUISITION EXAMINER (If applicable)	☒ AIR FORCE ADVISOR (If applicable)
NAME, GRADE, BR OF SVC, ORGN, COMD & LOCATION DAVID J. SEMON, Colonel, USAF SAF/AAO (HQ USAF) Washington DC 20330-1720	SIGNATURE *David J Semon*		DATE 28 May 97

AF FORM 707A, OCT 95 (REVERSE) (EF-V1) (PerFORM PRO)

FIELD GRADE OFFICER PERFORMANCE REPORT

ITEE IDENTIFICATION DATA *(Read AFI 36-2402 carefully before filling in any item)*			
AME *(Last, First, Middle Initial)* tterson, Robert B.	2. SSN	3. GRADE LT COL	4. DAFSC 16R4
PERIOD OF REPORT From: 11 May 97 Thru: 9 APR 98	6. NO. DAYS SUPERVISION 334	7. REASON FOR REPORT CRO	
ORGANIZATION, COMMAND, LOCATION White House Military Office, The White House, Washington, D.C. 20502 (ELM)			9. PAS CODE HH3VFRN1
UNIT MISSION DESCRIPTION			

rovides direct support to the President of the United States.

I. JOB DESCRIPTION

. DUTY TITLE:
Air Force Aide to the President

. KEY DUTIES, TASKS, AND RESPONSIBILITIES:
Emergency Actions Officer: develops and executes plans for contingencies ranging from medical emergencies to national security crises; safeguards and is responsible for the President's Emergency Satchel--"the Football." White House Military Office Operations Officer: coordinates employment of all military assets used in support of the President. Aide-de-Camp: military escort for the President at official functions, formal ceremonies and during travel; acts as personal assistant to the President during evenings, weekends, and visits to Camp David; other duties and functions as required by the President.

IV. IMPACT ON MISSION ACCOMPLISHMENT

- My senior Military Aide, Aide-de-Camp, and resident expert on emergency/contingency actions
  -- One of five elite military officers performing duties at my side from operational to ceremonial
  -- Performs as my personal aide on First Family sojourns to Camp David, Arkansas, Martha's Vineyard
  -- Primary Emergency Actions Officer for 100 Presidential events; trusted to advise me on our Nation's most sensitive contingency plans derived from diverse NSC, Secret Service and military assets
  Lead military advance planner for trips to seven foreign countries and 35 CONUS cities--deftly handled DoD support from communications, food service and medical, to watercraft, rotary, and fixed wing assets
- Poised, articulate, and witty public speaker--briefings on roles of military lauded by senior White House officials, U.S. Secret Service, White House Communications Agency, and 100 civilian staffers

V. PERFORMANCE FACTORS	DOES NOT MEET STANDARDS	MEETS STANDARDS
1. Job Knowledge Has knowledge required to perform duties effectively. Strives to improve knowledge. Applies knowledge to handle nonroutine situations.	☐	☒
2. Leadership Skills Sets and enforces standards. Motivates subordinates. Works well with others. Fosters teamwork. Displays initiative. Self-confident. Has respect and confidence of subordinates. Fair and consistent in evaluation of subordinates.	☐	☒
3. Professional Qualities Exhibits loyalty, discipline, dedication, integrity, honesty, and officership. Adheres to Air Force standards. Accepts personal responsibility. Is fair and objective.	☐	☒
4. Organizational Skills Plans, coordinates, schedules, and uses resources effectively. Schedules work for self and others equitably and effectively. Anticipates and solves problems. Meets suspenses.	☐	☒
5. Judgement and Decisions Makes timely and accurate decisions. Emphasizes logic in cision making. Retains composure in stressful situations. cognizes opportunities and acts to take advantage of them.	☐	☒
6. Communication Skills Listens, speaks, and writes effectively.	☐	☒

AF FORM 707A, OCT 95 *(EF -V1)* *(PerFORM PRO)*   PREVIOUS EDITION IS OBSOLETE.

My second field grade officer performance report as Air Force aide to the president.

VI. RATER OVERALL ASSESSMENT

Lt Col Buzz Patterson's performance as my Air Force Aide has been among the finest I have observed, marked by solid, quiet professionalism. He has been at my side for two years, traveling with me almost everywhere, and I will miss him. I count on his quick thinking and drive to tackle difficult logistical knots such as my Christmas trip to Bosnia. Faced with bad weather across the European continent, Buzz seamlessly directed the diversion of Air Force One and the relocation of our support airlift assets to meet us. He was the single military liaison for coordinating all ceremonial requirements for my state visits to the Netherlands, Denmark, Argentina and South Africa--all with poise and presence. The Air Force should be proud of Buzz and the truly unaffected manner in which he represented the military at the White House. Assign Buzz to the most demanding challenges. Select him for command immediately. Very bright future!

Last performance feedback was accomplished on: 27 Dec 97   *(consistent with the direction in AFI 36-2402.)*
(If not accomplished, state the reason)

NAME, GRADE, BR OF SVC, ORGN, COMD & LOCATION	DUTY TITLE		DATE
WILLIAM J. CLINTON, ES-1 The White House Washington, D.C. 20502	President of the United States		
	SSN	SIGNATURE	

VII. ADDITIONAL RATER OVERALL ASSESSMENT   CONCUR   NONCONCUR

He's a fine man. His work was outstanding. His potential is great.

NAME, GRADE, BR OF SVC, ORGN, COMD & LOCATION	DUTY TITLE		DATE
	SSN	SIGNATURE	

VIII. REVIEWER   CONCUR   NONCONCUR

Rater is also reviewer.

NAME, GRADE, BR OF SVC, ORGN, COMD & LOCATION	DUTY TITLE		DATE
	SSN	SIGNATURE	

Instructions

All: Recommendations must be based on performance and the potential based on that performance. Promotion recommendations are prohibited. Do not comment on completion of or enrollment in PME, advanced education, previous or anticipated promotion recommendations on AF Form 709, OER indorsement levels, family activities, marital status, race, sex, ethnic origin, age, or religion.

Rater: Focus your evaluation in Section IV on what the officer did, how well he or she did it and how the officer contributed to mission accomplishment. Write in concise "bullet" format. Your comments in Section VI may include recommendations for augmentation or assignment.

Additional Rater: Carefully review the rater's evaluation to ensure it is accurate, unbiased and uninflated. If you disagree, you may ask the rater to review his or her evaluation. You may not direct a change in the evaluation. If you still disagree with the rater, mark "NON-CONCUR" and explain. You may include recommendations for augmentation or assignment.

Reviewer: Carefully review the rater's and additional rater's ratings and comments. If their evaluations are accurate, unbiased and uninflated, mark the form "CONCUR" and sign the form. If you disagree with previous evaluators, you may ask them to review their evaluations. You may not direct them to change their appraisals. If you still disagree with the additional rater, mark "NONCONCUR" and explain in Section VIII. Do not use "NONCONCUR" simply to provide comments on the report.

IX. ACQUISITION EXAMINER/AIR FORCE ADVISOR *(Indicate applicable review by marking the appropriate box(es).)*		ACQUISITION EXAMINER *(If applicable)*	X	AIR FORCE ADVISOR *(If applicable)*
NAME, GRADE, BR OF SVC, ORGN, COMD & LOCATION DAVID J. SEMON, COL, USAF SAF/AA (HQ USAF)	SIGNATURE			DATE 8 May 98

AF FORM 707A, OCT 95 *(REVERSE) (EF-V** ¹Pe   ⁻M PRO)*

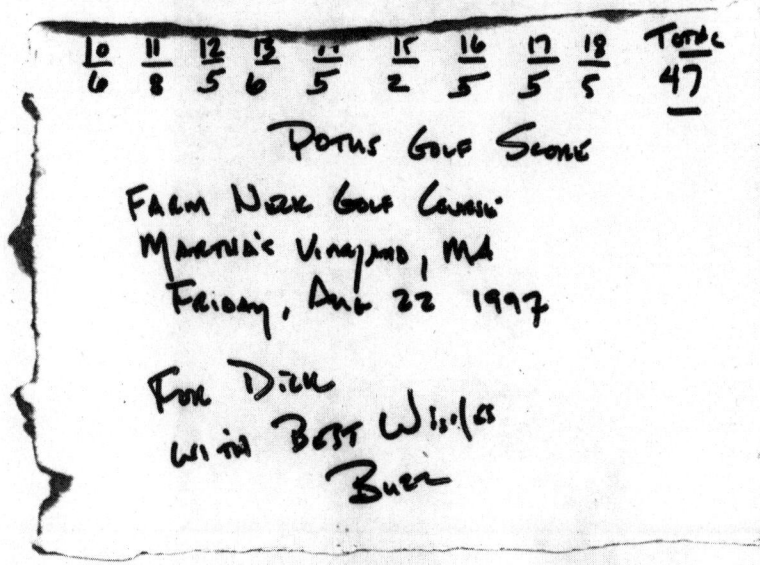

The boxed-lunch lid scorecard where the White House doctor and I kept Clinton's *real* golf score of the last nine holes during the presidential vacation to Martha's Vineyard in August 1997.

Notes

Prologue: Mission Aborted

1. R. Johanna McGeary, "Slamming Saddam Again," *Time,* September 16, 1996.

2. Andrew Phillips, "Why Saddam Won," *Macleans,* September 16, 1996.

3. John Farrell, "Iraq Fires at Jets; US Boosts Gulf Force; 'Not Playing Games,' Secretary Perry Says," *Boston Globe,* September 12, 1996.

Chapter Two: The Finger on the Nuclear Trigger

1. Jeffrey H. Birnbaum, *Madhouse: The Private Turmoil of Working for the President* (New York: Random House, 1996), 11.

2. J. Michael Waller, "No Nukes Pointed This Way? Think Again," *Washington Times,* July 6, 1998, A17.

3. Ibid.

4. Susan Schmidt, Peter Baker, and Toni Locy, "Clinton Accused of Urging Aide to Lie: Starr Probes Whether President Told Woman to Deny Alleged Affair to Jones's Lawyers," *Washington Post,* January 21, 1998.

Chapter Three: Hillary's "Football"

1. One significant exception was FBI agent Gary Aldrich in his book *Unlimited Access: An FBI Agent Inside the Clinton White House* (Washington, D.C.: Regnery, 1996), though his primary concern, like mine, was with the administration's shocking disdain for national security.

2. Paul Johnson, "The Rogue in the White House," *Esquire,* June 1997, 66.

3. I was never deeply involved in presidential issues vis-à-vis China, but some of the president's critics on Capitol Hill thought, before the terrorist

attacks of September 11, 2001, that Clinton's legacy was selling out American security to the Communist Chinese. See, for instance, the two books by congressional defense experts Edward Timperlake and William C. Triplett II, *Year of the Rat: How Bill Clinton Compromised U.S. Security for Chinese Cash* (Washington, D.C.: Regnery, 1998) and *Red Dragon Rising: Communist China's Military Threat to America* (Washington, D.C.: Regnery, 1999).

4. John Berthoud and Demian Brady, "Bill Clinton: America's Best-Traveled President: A Study of Presidential Travel: 1953–2001," *National Taxpayers Union Policy Paper #104,* March 16, 2001.

5. Ibid.

6. Josh Mercer, "Waste & Abuse," *Insight on the News,* July 26, 1999, 23.

7. Larry Craig, "Africa, Chile, China...Next Outer Mongolia?" United States Senate Republican Policy Committee, September 22, 1999.

8. Robert Goodrich, "Top Scott Officers Say Clinton Has Overused Planes," *St. Louis Post-Dispatch,* January 10, 1999.

9. Ibid.

10. Colonel David Hackworth, "The High Flying Clintons," NewsMax.com, March 28, 2000.

CHAPTER FOUR: FEAR AND LOATHING

1. Susan Fey, "Hubbell Employer Flew on Air Force One: Beaumont Lawyer Among 56 Donors on Plane," *Dallas Morning News,* April 15, 1997, 6A.

2. Letter written by Bill Clinton to Colonel Eugene Holmes, 1969.

3. Barton Gellman, "Turning an About Face into a Forward March: Clinton and Military Begin to Move in Stride," *Washington Post,* April 1, 1993.

4. Kenneth T. Walsh, Bruce B. Auster, and Tim Zimmerman, "Clinton's Warrior Woes," *U.S. News & World Report,* March 15, 1993, 22–24.

5. Gellman, "Turning an About Face into a Forward March."

6. General Ronald R. Fogleman, "The Early Retirement of Gen. Ronald R. Fogleman, Chief of Staff, United States Air Force," *Aerospace Power Journal,* Spring 2001.

7. Wesley Pruden, "The Uniform Insult at the White House," *Washington Times,* April 2, 1993, A4.

8. Michael R. Gordon, "General Ousted for Derisive Remarks About President," *New York Times,* June 19, 1993, 9.

Chapter Five: National Defense or Social Petri Dish?

1. Center for Military Readiness, "'Legacy Project' Launches Spin Campaign to Obscure Clinton Record on Military Readiness," January 24, 2002.

2. Robert Bork, *Slouching Towards Gomorrah* (New York: Regan Books, 1996), 88.

3. "Gays-Military Chronology," Associated Press News Service, December 22, 1993.

4. See Brian Mitchell, *Women in the Military* (Washington, D.C.: Regnery, 1998).

5. Richard Grenier, "Bill Clinton's Armchair Warriors," *Washington Times,* November 18, 1997.

6. Ibid.

7. NewsMax.com Articles, Center for Military Readiness, "Pregnancy/Family Policies," July 2000.

8. Rowan Scarborough, "Dropout Rate High for Women on Ships: Navy Study Finds Readiness Woes," *Washington Times,* March 8, 1999, A1.

9. Paul Richter, "Army Seeks Sweat Equity in Wake of Sex Harassment; Military: Women Face Fitness Tests More on Par with Men After Report Cites Male Perception of 'Lesser' Soldiers," *Los Angeles Times,* September 14, 1997, A1.

10. J. Michael Waller, "Policy Disaster," *Insight on the News,* November 13, 2000, 10.

11. Rowan Scarborough, "Record Deployments Take Toll on Military: 48 Missions in '90s Totaling $30 Billion Strain Personnel, Equipment, Study Finds," *Washington Times,* March 28, 2000, A6. See also, Geoff Metcalf, "The Excrement of Propaganda," WorldNetDaily, March 29, 1999.

12. Clark Simmons, "Must Build Military Readiness," *Times-Picayune*, December 18, 1994, B10.

13. David Hackworth, "Clinton Can Undo the Damages in Military Morale," *Newsweek*, June 28, 1993, 24–25.

14. Al Santoli, "They're Fighting to Stay Above the Poverty Line," *Parade*, May 28, 1995.

CHAPTER SIX: CNN DIPLOMACY

1. Metcalf, "The Excrement of Propaganda."

2. Alex Morrison and Kevin A. O'Brien, "U.S. Retreating from Peacekeeping," *Hamilton Spectator,* May 24, 1994.

3. Lawrence T. Di Rita, "Fiction and Fact: The Clinton Speech on Haiti," Heritage Foundation, September 16, 1994.

CHAPTER SEVEN: THE WAR ON TERRORISM

1. Robert Graham and Quentin Peel, "The U.S. Attack on Libya: The 10-Day Countdown to Reagan's Decision to Order Jets In," *Financial Times* (London), April 16, 1986, 2.

2. Byron York, "Clinton Has No Clothes," *National Review* 53, no. 24 (December 17, 2001), 35.

3. Steven Emerson, Testimony Before the Subcommittee on Africa of the House International Relations Committee, April 6, 1995.

4. Bassem Mroue, "Saudi Militant: Extremists Fought U.S. in Somalia," Associated Press, November 26, 1996.

5. Sam Vincent Meddis, "Terrorism Brushes U.S. Again," *USA Today,* March 9, 1995.

6. Norman Kempster, "Truck Bomb Kills 23 Americans at an Air Base in Saudi Arabia," *Los Angeles Times,* June 26, 1996.

7. Bill Clinton, "Americans Who Made a Difference," Speech at Eglin AFB Memorial Service, June 30, 1996.

8. York, "Clinton Has No Clothes."

9. Russell Watson and John Barry, "Our Target Was Terror," *Newsweek,* August 31, 1998, 24.

10. York, "Clinton Has No Clothes."

11. Susan Page, "Why Clinton Failed to Stop bin Laden," *USA Today,* November 12, 2001.

12. For a good discussion of this, and for the broader history of America's intelligence failures over the past several decades, see Bill Gertz's *Breakdown: How America's Intelligence Failures Led to September 11* (Washington, D.C.: Regnery, 2002). Bill Gertz, the much respected defense and national security reporter for the *Washington Times,* wrote two other books that provide an excellent discussion of the dangerous foreign policy, especially as regards terrorism and direct threats to American national security, of the Clinton administration. See his books *Betrayal: How the Clinton Administration Undermined American Security* (Washington, D.C.: Regnery, 1999) and *The China Threat: How the People's Republic Targets America* (Washington, D.C.: Regnery, 2000).

Acknowledgments

First and foremost, my sincere thanks and appreciation to the many men and women with whom I have served in my twenty years in the U.S. Air Force. The faces, the places, and our shared circumstances will live with me forever. Most notably, I salute the men and women who shouldered the presidential military aide responsibilities with me. Colonel Mike Mudd, United States Army; Major Chuck Raderstorf, United States Marine Corps; Commander John Richardson, United States Navy; and Lieutenant Commander June Ryan, United States Coast Guard, were the first team I joined. Lieutenant Colonel Dana Pittard, USA; Major Duffy White, USMC; Lieutenant Commander Wes Huey, USN; and Lieutenant Commander Graham Stowe, USCG, were my brethren and confidants when I departed. I'd go to war with any one of them, anywhere, anytime. They are our country's "finest of the finest."

My sincere thanks to the wonderful folks at Regnery Publishing. This book would not have happened if Mr. Al Regnery had not taken a chance on an otherwise unpublished author "wanna-be" with no résumé. Sincere thanks to him for giving me the opportunity and for his patience throughout this project. Through him, I was blessed with the privilege to work with Mr. Al Santoli and Mr. Harry Crocker. Al was my coach, counselor, and supporter throughout the developmental stages in spite of his demanding projects with the American Foreign Policy Council. Harry took over, smoothed the rough edges, and taught me how invaluable a really good editor in chief is. Special thanks, also, to Ms. Miriam Moore, Harry Crocker's assistant editor, and to Ms. Mahlet Getachew, Al Santoli's administrative assistant, who were absolutely essential in offering their unbiased, non-military scrutiny of each and every word.

Due to a strange set of employment circumstances, much of this book was written in a tiny hotel room at the Ramada Limited in Valdosta, Georgia. Many thanks to Mrs. Evelyn Webb and her staff for making my eight-month stay there a "home away from home."

Finally, I must thank Mr. Ben Schemmer, a family friend, a published author, and a literary agent in his own right. While this project was germinating, Ben taught me the basics of the publishing industry, helped me to understand the business of writing, and consistently encouraged me. He did so as a personal favor. Without his inspiration and insight, this book would simply not exist.

I've been blessed in so many ways by so very many people. To all my friends and family, thank you for all you mean to me.

The views expressed in this book are my own and are not necessarily shared by any of the people or organizations I have thanked.

Index